CONTENTS

TITAN EDITORIAL
Editor Jonathan Wilkins
Group Editor Jake Devine
Art Director Oz Browne
Editorial Assistant Ibraheem Kazi
Copy Editor Phoebe Hedges
Assistant Editor Calum Collins
Production Controller Kelly Fenlon
Production Controller Caterina Falqui
Production Manager Jackie Flook
Sales & Circulation Manager Steve Tothill
Marketing Coordinator Lauren Noding
Publicity & Sales Coordinator
Alexandra Iciek
Publicity Manager Will O'Mullane
Digital & Marketing Manager Jo Teather
Head of Creative & Business Development
Duncan Baizley
Publishing Directors Ricky Claydon
& John Dziewiatkowski
Group Operations Director Alex Ruthen
Executive Vice President Andrew Sumner
Publishers Vivian Cheung & Nick Landau

DISTRIBUTION
U.S. Newsstand: Total Publisher
Services, Inc.
John Dziewiatkowski, 630-851-7683
U.S. Newsstand Distribution: Curtis
Circulation Company

PRINTED IN CHINA

U.S. Bookstore Distribution:
The News Group
U.S. Direct Sales: Diamond Comic
Distributors

For more info on advertising contact
adinfo@titanemail.com

Marvel Studios' *Black Panther: Wakanda
Forever The Official Movie Special*
Published October 2023 by Titan Magazines,
a division of Titan Publishing Group Limited,
144 Southwark Street, London, SE1 0UP.
For sale in the U.S. and Canada.
ISBN: 9781787738720

Thanks to Kevin Pearl, Samantha Keane,
Rodney Vallo, Shiho Tilley, and Eugene
Paraszczuk at Disney.

Authorized User. No part of this publication
may be reproduced, stored in a retrival

system, or transmitted, in any form or by any
means, without the prior written permission
of the publisher. A CIP catalogue record for
this title is available from the British Library.

10 9 8 7 6 5 4 3 2 1

DISNEY PUBLISHING WORLDWIDE
Global Magazines, Comics and Partworks

Publisher Lynn Waggoner

Editorial Director Bianca Coletti

Editorial Team
Guido Frazzini (Director, Comics),
Stefano Ambrosio (Executive Editor,
New IP), Carlotta Quattrocolo (Executive
Editor, Franchise), Camilla Vedove (Senior
Manager, Editorial Development), Behnoosh
Khalili (Senior Editor), Julie Dorris (Senior
Editor), Kendall Tamer (Assistant Editor),
Cristina Casas (Assistant Editor),
Enrico Soave (Senior Designer)

Art
Ken Shue (VP, Global Art), Roberto Santillo
(Creative Director), Marco Ghiglione
(Creative Manager), Manny Mederos
(Senior Illustration Manager, Comics
and Magazines), Stefano Attardi (Illustration
Manager)

Portfolio Management
Olivia Ciancarelli (Director)

Business & Marketing
Mariantonietta Galla (Senior
Manager, Franchise),
Virpi Korhonen (Editorial Manager)

Contributing Editor
Giulia Vielmi

Text
Simon Beecroft
Graphic Design and Photo Editing
Nicoletta Valentini, Falcinelli & Co.

Thanks to
Sarah Beers, Kristy Amornkul, Adam Davis
Julio Palacol, Jacqueline Ryan-Rudolph
Capri Ciulla, Erika Denton, Jeff Willis

Dig into recent events in Wakanda and get ready for the explosive present.

WAKANDA'S NEXT CHAPTER

The secretive African nation of Wakanda, with its fabulous blend of ancient and futuristic technology, is facing a difficult hour. King T'Challa, the Black Panther, is dead—suddenly and unexpectedly. T'Challa came to the throne after his father, King T'Chaka, was killed by a bomb while making a speech at the signing of the Sokovia Accords to limit the power of Super Heroes. T'Chaka had agreed with 117 world governments that the power of secretive government agencies such as S.H.I.E.L.D. and private organizations such as the Avengers should be curbed. He had been only too aware that the Avengers, foiling a terrorist plot in Lagos, had accidentally caused the death of Wakandans working on an outreach mission.

T'Challa's first act as King was to bring his father's killer to justice—the Super Villain Baron Zemo. He also went after arms dealer Ulysses Klaue, who had stolen vibranium from Wakanda in the past: in the wrong hands, this rare and virtually indestructible metal, which provides the power source for Wakanda's incredibly advanced technology, could prove unimaginably destructive. T'Challa also fought off a challenge to the throne from his own cousin, Erik Killmonger. He united the tribes of Wakanda, vowing to end his country's isolationism, work with the world's governments, and share his nation's knowledge and resources.

BLACK PANTHER'S EMBLEM, WITH A GOLD RING SYMBOLIZING ROYALTY.

As Black Panther, T'Challa fought alongside the Avengers in their battles against Thanos. When Thanos gained control of the Infinity Stones, he extinguished half of all life in the universe with a mere snap of his fingers: among those affected by the Blip were T'Challa and his brilliant sister, Shuri. After a five-year period of world turmoil, known as the Blip, the Avengers managed to bring back the victims, including T'Challa and Shuri. But after T'Challa's actual death, Wakanda entered a period of deep mourning. With T'Challa's mother, Ramonda, on the throne, the Wakandans are striving to understand what their next chapter will be—when, suddenly, a new threat arrives from beneath the waves: Namor and the Talokanil. Despite the absence of a Black Panther—their warrior king—to guide and lead them, the Wakandan nation must come together to face new challenges.

Meet Wakanda's royal family and key members of the ruling tribal council.

WHO'S WHO: WAKANDAN LEADERS

Queen Ramonda

PORTRAYED BY

ANGELA BASSETT

Mother of recently deceased King T'Challa, Queen Ramonda has a heavy burden as she takes the reins of power as leader of Wakanda. She must manage her own grief and that of her daughter, Princess Shuri.

Princess Shuri

PORTRAYED BY

LETITIA WRIGHT

Shuri is the Princess of Wakanda and lead scientist of the Wakandan Design Group. She will be forced to overcome the grief of losing her brother T'Challa when Wakanda's borders are breached by an unexpected threat.

M'Baku

PORTRAYED BY

WINSTON DUKE

M'Baku is the leader of the Jabari Tribe and an avid traditionalist who rejects the technological advancements of Wakanda. He finds himself in a unique position of leadership without a Black Panther.

Wakanda is protected by elite warriors. Let's learn about them.

WHO'S WHO: WAKANDA'S PROTECTORS

Okoye

PORTRAYED BY

DANAI GURIRA

The general of the Dora Milaje and leader of Wakanda's armies, Okoye is the nation's fiercest warrior. However, she will be challenged like never before when she battles both a foe beyond her strength and the very traditions of Wakanda itself.

Ayo

PORTRAYED BY

FLORENCE KASUMBA

Ayo is the Dora Milaje Security Chief and General Okoye's right hand. She is adept at disguise and armed with a traditional vibranium spear.

Aneka

PORTRAYED BY

MICHAELA COEL

Aneka is a member of the Dora Milaje who goes on overseas missions with Okoye and Ayo. She tests out Shuri's new tech in the field and flies alongside the Princess in her Sunbird flying ship.

Nakia

PORTRAYED BY

LUPITA NYONG'O

The former war dog has stayed true to her word after the events of *Black Panther* by helping those in need outside of Wakanda. Nakia will have to put her political differences aside and return to Wakanda when a new threat arises.

A brief introduction to some of Wakanda's new foes and allies.

WHO'S WHO: TALOKANIL AND OTHERS

Namor

PORTRAYED BY

TENOCH HUERTA MEJÌA

Namor is the ruler of Talokan, a breakaway civilization descended from ancient Mayans and hidden in the depths of the ocean. Born with winged ankles, incredible strength, and the ability to breath both underwater and on land, he will stop at nothing to protect his people and preserve their culture.

Namora

PORTRAYED BY

MABEL CADENA

A highly skilled fighter, Namora is a precise and ruthless warrior whose skills with a harpoon and connection with the creatures of the deep make her an invaluable member of Namor's army.

Attuma

PORTRAYED BY

ALEX LIVINALLI

The strongest general in Namor's army, Attuma is brash and a little reckless, and isn't afraid to defy orders if it means finding an opponent worthy of battle.

Riri Williams

PORTRAYED BY

DOMINIQUE THORNE

A young, brilliant MIT student who has a passion for engineering, Riri Williams' life takes an unexpected turn when a school project brings the Wakandans and a dangerous foe to her doorstep.

The filmmakers and cast reflect on the great Chadwick Boseman and how his passing affected the making of *Black Panther: Wakanda Forever.*

HONORING CHADWICK BOSEMAN

FOREVER
11.11.22

ABOVE TOP: THE TEASER POSTER REVEALED AT SAN DIEGO COMIC-CON IN JULY 2022.
ABOVE: M'BAKU AT THE FUNERAL OF T'CHALLA.

Ryan Coogler (Writer and Director):
"Chadwick's passing affected us all profoundly. It was shocking and emotionally devastating. Chad was very much our artistic partner in this project. I would spend time with him, just he and I, talking about where we wanted the character and the story to go, and how much he admired the other characters and the actors who portrayed them."

Nate Moore (Producer):
"First, there was just the reality of losing the man. The film was secondary to figuring out how we move forward as friends and colleagues of his. There wasn't a lot of discussion early on about the film. As the shock of Chad's passing started to fade a bit and be less present, we began to discuss whether it would be right to move forward with a film without our central actor who really created that character for film audiences."

Coogler:
"We had written a screenplay for Chadwick before we were aware of his illness, but it was very much from T'Challa's perspective. So now we had to think about what the world would be like if his character passed away. It became a different movie, because T'Challa is so consequential to everything that happens in Wakanda."

Ruth Carter (Costume Designer):
"Initially, we thought of ways that the film could be done with Chadwick, using outtakes from the first film. But Ryan didn't want to do that. The first film was a father and son story. In this film, there's a mother and daughter story. Ryan and Joe Robert chose not to avoid the subject of loss and grief, but to use it as a way of getting into the story itself."

Joe Robert Cole (Co-writer):
"Where we landed seemed to fit where everybody was emotionally. We were all in agreement that we didn't want to recast the film and that we wanted to find a way to speak to the wonderful man Chadwick was. It felt like the right way to honor him."

Moore:
"Our approach was to deal with T'Challa's passing like Chadwick's passing happened in real life. The passing that you couldn't have seen coming, that had very little to do with someone being heroic or non-heroic. This approach seemed more honest. We've all lost people in ways that are surprising and couldn't be anticipated. The film then becomes a meditation of how you fill that gap."

Cole:
"The first film was about Chad's character dealing with the loss of his father, stepping into his father's shoes, and leading the kingdom in a new direction in a new world. And this film does something very similar, except now it's Ramonda and Shuri dealing with the loss of T'Challa and guiding Wakanda forward."

Coogler:
"As we refocused the film onto Shuri and Ramonda, a new theme of grief and loss surfaced, and how you move forward after losing someone that meant so much to you."

Cole:
"Shuri and Ramonda's relationship takes center stage and we explore that dynamic. Ramonda has dealt with grief before, having lost her husband, T'Chaka. She also lost Shuri and T'Challa in the Blip and then experienced their return, so she has a unique point of view."

Angela Bassett (Ramonda):
"I think my character was the first one to actually—and I'm getting chills—sit in the seat where Chadwick sat as king. I now sit there as Ramonda, as queen—and those are big shoes to fill. But I felt his presence—his spirit was on that set with us."

Alex Livinalli (Attuma):
"Chadwick was more than just an actor. He was family to everyone in the cast and crew; not even just that, but to the Black film community and the fans. This movie is a celebration for everyone that's seen Chadwick or knows him."

Bassett:
"Chadwick was an incredibly special, unique, forward-thinking human being. He gave his all. He knew exactly what this world, this story, and these images meant to the world. In telling this story, we together—both on screen and off screen, audience and actors and those who are behind the actors, cast and crew— we're able to honor him together."

Moore:
"I think this movie has a chance, not only to celebrate the loss of the man, both the character and the performer, but also to allow audiences to grieve and move on and see that there is still room for hope, joy, fun, and laughter even past that."

RAMONDA AND SHURI WEAR WHITE AT T'CHALLA'S FUNERAL TO GRIEVE HIS PASSING BUT ALSO TO CELEBRATE HIS LIFE AND MARK HIS ASCENSION TO THE ANCESTRAL PLANE.

Join the
filmmakers in
a discussion
about the
state of
Wakanda in
the movie
and the
ongoing
political
consequences
of decisions
that T'Challa
made in the
first film.

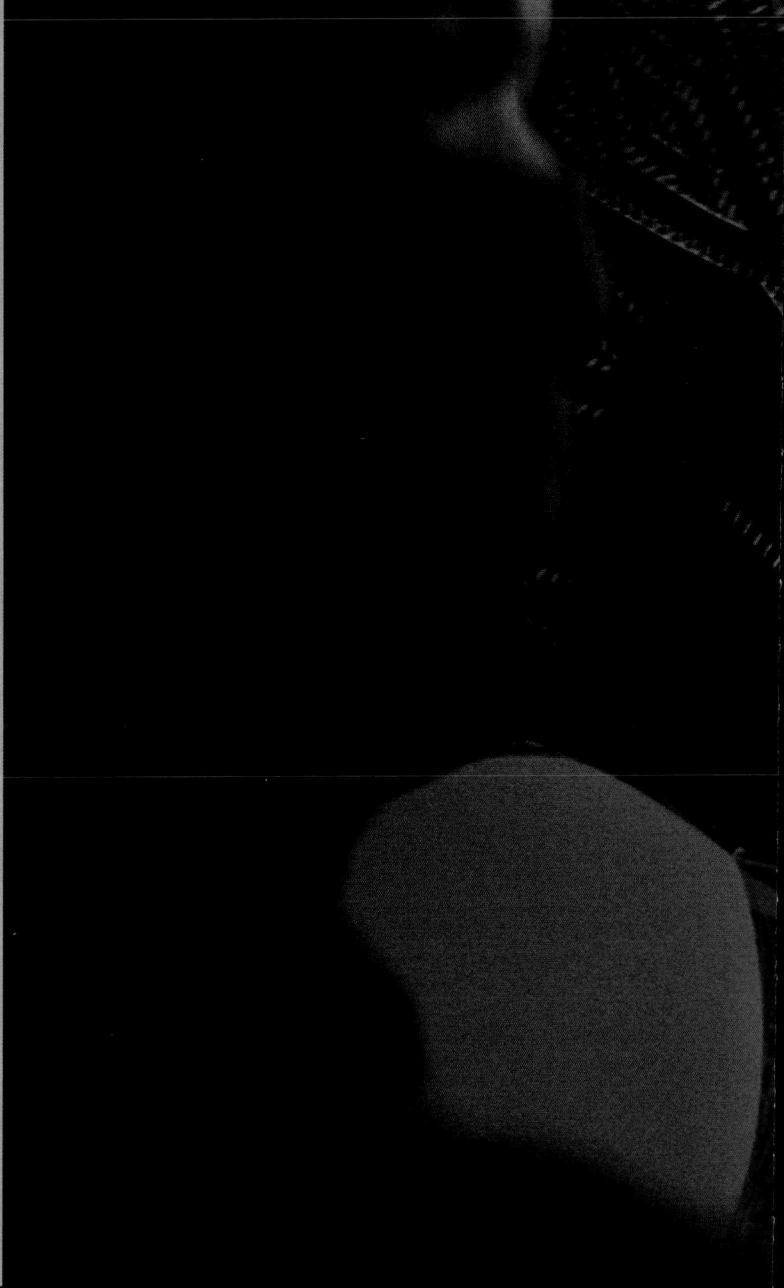

REVISITING
WAKANDA

Joe Robert Cole (Co-writer):
Black Panther: Wakanda Forever picks up post-Blip. During the Blip, T'Challa and Shuri were gone, and Ramonda took the throne again. Wakanda continues to be at odds with the world because of its isolationism and its control of the advanced technology that vibranium makes possible.

Nate Moore (Producer):
Queen Ramonda is dealing with the fallout of the passing of her son, T'Challa, who was also the Black Panther, the nation's defender. She is also dealing with the political decisions he made in sharing vibranium and that technology with some parts of the world and not others. That decision has made Wakanda a target on the global stage because Queen Ramonda has steadfastly refused to share vibranium with all the big powers.

Angela Bassett (Ramonda):
The world is aware of Wakanda; aware of the resources that we have and how important Wakanda is to the world. They're greedy for it. You don't know who you can trust.

Ryan Coogler (Writer and Director):
T'Challa made a choice that he was comfortable with, because he thought he would be around to handle it. Unfortunately, in the storytelling—and, even more unfortunately in reality, with the loss of Chadwick—T'Challa doesn't live to make sure Wakanda's transition onto the global stage is handled properly—and also that his nation doesn't get into conflicts it can't handle.

Cole:
Post-Blip, the world sees Wakanda in a different light. With T'Challa's passing, there's no Black Panther. The world is desperate to level the playing field and get access to vibranium, which becomes a big trigger point in the new movie. One of the things that made the first film special was that we embraced lots of different points of view. The Wakandans were constantly working through where they stand in the world, which made for richer scenes. We see a lot more of this in the new movie. There's the internal politics, the familial relationships, and the relationships between the Wakandan tribal leaders.

RAMONDA VISITS THE UNITED NATIONS.

Moore:

Many Wakandans feel like their nation shouldn't have been made as public as it has, and all of the countries outside of Wakanda feel like Wakanda's not doing enough to share their technology, to share their resources. So T'Challa's decision has put him in the cross hairs of the Western public and the people inside his country. With T'Challa's passing, Ramonda is left with a legacy that maybe she wouldn't have chosen and she's forced to navigate those waters. Wakanda feels a little bit unprotected. The outside world feels like they can be a bit more aggressive because they know that Wakanda's Super Hero king has gone. So Wakanda is having to play more defense than it ever has before because everybody knows exactly what the nation has. That's where Wakanda finds itself before a new player enters the stage and flips the board for everybody.

Cole:

Ramonda had been more concerned with nations that have military power and have a history of exploiting other places for resources. She did not know about this nation that was in the water; she didn't see this problem coming. And, boy, does it come hard in our film! When Namor, the leader of the mysterious underwater nation of Talokan, finds his way into their country and walks out of the river up to Queen Ramonda, this immediately causes a big stir. We see how the Wakandans relate to an external threat from the world outside their border, and there are lots of points of view on how to deal with Namor.

FAR LEFT: M'BAKU SITS ON WAKANDA'S RULING COUNCIL.
CENTER LEFT: RAMONDA ADDRESSES THE UN.
LEFT: SHURI VISITS THE WAKANDAN ANCESTRAL PLANE.

Let the filmmakers be your guide to the behind-the-scenes story of how Namor and the underwater world of Talokan were introduced into the movie.

DISCOVERING TALOKAN

Nate Moore (Producer):

There were very few ideas that were as interesting as introducing Namor and Talokan into the world of Wakanda. These two nations have a ton of things in common and many things that are completely different—that dichotomy is what makes the relationship really fascinating. In the comics, Wakanda and Talokan have gone to war multiple times. In our storytelling, it's the fact that Wakanda isn't giving vibranium to the outside world that starts to put Talokan on the map.

Joe Robert Cole (Co-writer):

Namor and Talokan rely on vibranium, which Wakanda didn't even realize was out in the world. It's that discovery by the surface world that there is vibranium in the oceans that draws them in direct conflict with Namor and his people. All of a sudden Wakanda finds itself in between this new underwater power and some of the surface countries that want to steal the vibranium from Wakanda.

Ryan Coogler (Writer and Director):

Just as we wanted Wakanda to feel like a real place, we knew that we needed to build a history for Talokan, too. With Wakanda, the nation was able to stay put and avoid colonization. But what if another place had to leave and was forced to go somewhere else and that was the defining difference between these two places? Namor had to be somebody who would've been around at that the time that his people transitioned, because in the comics he's very long-lived. That's what pushed us toward Mesoamerican culture.

Cole:

In the comics, Namor's Atlantis is very much influenced by ancient Rome with its stone column architecture. But Ryan wanted to place it in a culture and a region that was not utilized very much in film and that would allow the characters then to have a cultural specificity of their own.

Ruth Carter (Costume Designer):

I first started researching ancient Greece, and there was a whole other story surrounding Atlantis. But in order to make our story unique, we wanted to center it in Mesoamerica and create the story of a people that was conquered by the Spaniards, and use that history. So, it was important that we gave it a traditional name that was real to that culture, and that's how we came up with Talokan and the Talokanil. That was based on research and talking to historians, and coming up with the concept.

NAMOR AND THE TALOKANIL EMERGE FROM THE DEPTHS. ART BY PHIL SAUNDERS.

Moore:

In Mayan mythology, Talokan is the underworld and the people then become the Talokanil. They were forced to rebuild their society underwater, out of the eyes of the Western world, because they knew that if they went to the surface they would be killed. Hannah Beachler [Production Designer], with help from our consultant, Dr. Gerardo Aldana [Professor of Anthropology and Chicano Studies at the University of California, Santa Barbara], created an underwater city built mostly with stone, but couched in architectural styles, colors, and iconography from the Mayan civilization.

Coogler:

In pulling from Mesoamerican culture, we've been able to incorporate some of those influences into Namor's traditional design. So you will see Namor put on a headdress or an incredible necklace. Dr. Aldana helped to guide us in a way that was accurate—as accurate as it needed to be for our MCU [Marvel Cinematic Universe] storytelling. Of course, we get into fantastical stuff like vibranium and magical discoveries that enable people to breathe underwater. But we started from a historical and archaeological base.

Moore:

The Mayan civilization was incredibly advanced in Mesoamerica for centuries up until the Spanish conquistadores arrived. The story of Namor's people is that, in an attempt to flee genocide, famine, and disease, they took what amounts to the Talokan version of the Heart-Shaped Herb—a vibranium-enriched flower that grows in the water—that allows them to live and breathe underwater. Namor's mother and all of the Mayan villagers who lived with her managed to escape the devastation caused by the Spanish conquistadores by going underwater and starting what would become Talokan.

Cole:

Talokan is a hidden civilization that wants to remain hidden. By exposing itself and vibranium to the world, Wakanda has opened up a vulnerability for Talokan to be exposed as well. There is a scientist who has created a vibranium detector and Namor comes to task Ramonda with finding the scientist, casting blame on Wakanda for causing the issue. When they find the scientist, she turns out to be a nineteen-year-old MIT student, Riri Williams, and this changes everything in terms of her connection with Shuri and it really turns our story on its ear.

Director and Co-Screenwriter Ryan Coogler reveals some of the challenges of making the film, and what he's most excited about bringing to the screen in *Black Panther: Wakanda Forever*.

RYAN COOGLER
WRITER/DIRECTOR

"*Black Panther* was about the struggle to move on after the death of a father. This film explores the relationship between Ramonda and Shuri."

How did Chadwick's passing affect the sequel?
It was going to be Chad's movie in a way that even the first one, which was more of an ensemble, wasn't. We were planning to bring all the characters back, with new characters, and do a really cool, interesting thing with the villain—but it was all going to be firmly rooted in T'Challa's perspective for the most part. Chad was looking forward to doing it. When he passed away, we really had to take time to grieve for the person whom we knew. It took a lot of work to come up with the screenplay that we ended up going forward with. When we shifted it, we realized that this would be a whole new thing, even though we might be dealing with this same antagonist and maybe similar situation.

What is the setup for the new movie?
Black Panther was about the struggle to move on after the passing of a father. T'Challa had to reckon with what kind of man he was going to be. This film explores the relationship between Ramonda and Shuri. We know Ramonda's character as the mom of the king, but in this film she's the queen of Wakanda, as well as being the mother to her daughter, Shuri. We see what she was going through and her perspective on the loss of T'Challa, which is very different from Shuri's perspective. When the Blip happened, Shuri and T'Challa disappeared, but Ramonda was left. Her character has had this really complex emotional experience of losing both her kids, then being reunited with them, and losing one again. She is trying to give Shuri some emotional insight into this.

What made you decide to bring Namor into this film?
We're really excited to portray this character in the film. Comic book fans will know him; he's one of the oldest Marvel characters [first introduced in 1939, when Marvel Comics was still known as Timely Comics]. His very appearance shows that Wakanda is not as safe as it thought it was. In the comics, Black Panther has a really fun rogues' gallery. He has conflicts with Ulysses Klaue, Erik Killmonger, Dr. Doom, Kraven the Hunter, the X-Men, and many others. But the conflicts he has with Namor are the ones that stick in your head. These tended to be the most complex and are the most fun, with the greatest lines of dialogue. In the first *Black Panther* film,

A CLOSE EXCHANGE BETWEEN SHURI AND QUEEN RAMONDA.

LETITIA WRIGHT AS SHURI WEARS THE NEW BLACK PANTHER SUIT WITH ITS DISTINCTIVE SILVER AND GOLD ACCENTS.

T'Challa tells Klaue, "Every breath you take is mercy from me." But actually, in the comics, Black Panther said that to Namor. These characters had so much in common and for some reason just despised each other.

How do you figure out all the different character arcs in one cohesive story?

I work with screenwriter Joe Robert Cole, along with our assistants, and Nate Moore, our producer at Marvel Studios, who was there on the first movie as well. We card it out [using index cards to represent each scene or story moment, so they can be moved around in order to find the best flow of scenes to tell the story] and we talk about it. We discuss what's not working, whether what everybody's doing is believable, or if we're losing the audience. Sometimes we'll have somebody do something because it's cool but it might not make a whole lot of sense. We're constantly tracking and monitoring that. You don't want to watch a movie where the characters are the same at the end as they were when they started, because you would feel like you wasted your time. The characters in Black Panther are somewhat mythological and archetypal. But you want them to feel like real people and see them challenged. You want to see them go to places that maybe you didn't expect. When you achieve a proper arc, you really gain the affection of an audience, because everybody wants to see characters go through something that's consequential.

What are some of the production challenges?

Before we started shooting, we pre-visualized as much as we could from the storyboards. We figured out what we would need in each shot. We always spend a lot of time making sure the VFX [visual effects] can get off to the right start. We want to have everything ready before the actors arrive on set. The sets are big and we have to make sure we spread our budget so we can get everything we need. We have to figure out what's going to go to visual effects and how many stunt players we need—and how many of these stunt players need to be water players! We have to figure out how many weapons we needed and what they should look like, as well as costumes. We have to get the script dialed in so that we're not biting off more than we can chew, and not shooting scenes that we're not going to use. Amid all that, we must still take time to take a step back and make sure that we're doing right by Chadwick, for the people who loved him, and the audience. The ship has to be headed in the right direction, because you know that it'll be hard to change course once all the actors land and we get cameras up. Our first day of filming was July 7, 2021, a Thursday. It was the UN scene, with Angela Bassett as Ramonda, shot right here in Atlanta.

ABOVE TOP: LED BY NAMORA, SHURI EXPERIENCES THE WONDERS OF TALOKAN.
ABOVE: TENOCH HUERTA MEJÍA (NAMOR) ON SET WITH DIRECTOR RYAN COOGLER.

Joe Robert Cole co-wrote *Black Panther* with Ryan Coogler and returns to co-write the sequel. He talks to us about underwater worlds, creative freedom, and much more.

JOE ROBERT COLE

CO-WRITER

"We have really wonderful actors and we want to give them something to work with. We want them to know where they're going and that way the collaborative process becomes a richer one."

What excites you about Black Panther: Wakanda Forever?
The magic of the Marvel Cinematic Universe is how it just seems to continue to expand in a really rich, fun, and exciting way. You really look forward to following these characters beyond where they're introduced, whether it's in a show or elsewhere. One example is the screen debut of Riri Williams, played by Dominique Thorne. Like Shuri, Riri is a genius engineer and inventor, and they are similar ages, but Riri obviously has a very different point of view, as an African American coming from the south side of Chicago. Having grown up working on car parts and making something out of nothing, she's more into combustion technology than the kind of high-tech stuff that Shuri works on. There is this great oil-and-water thing that exists between the two of them that makes their scenes kind of crackle and work well. I mean, we're just introducing her and there is so much else that will unfold later on.

During the writing process, are you thinking about fleshing out every character's arc?
It's a case of respecting each character and giving them a purpose, a reason they're in the story. We have to decide on the story we want to tell for that character, where we want the characters to go, how they relate to the larger theme of grief, and how it all meshes together to form the whole. We have really wonderful actors and we want to give them something to work with. We want them to know where they're going and that way the collaborative process becomes a richer one. The characters are so cool, all with very distinct personalities and points of view. It's a really fulfilling challenge to find those journeys for everyone.

How did you write Namor's underwater world?
The scale of Talokan is just unbelievable, with the beauty of the Mayan civilization re-created underwater. We really leaned on our historians and the culture advisers to help us to create an authentic undersea world. We tried to think scientifically about how the culture from the surface would translate to below—and what it would mean spiritually; how the Talokanil would look at their gods. All of these things have been baked into the creation of Talokan, which is really, really exciting.

DOMINIQUE THORNE AS RIRI WILLIAMS IN HER IRONHEART ARMOR.

Do you enjoy the creative freedom of working on a big-budget MCU movie?

Yes! You really have the freedom to think big and let your mind go wherever it wants to go. If it's a great idea and it works within the story, then usually it finds its way into the film. It's very liberating. There are so many smart, creative people —the visual development team, the stunt team—just everyone involved is part of the soup, so you don't have to be the "genius." You're really a part of the team that is working together to make something great. It's really fun and enriching to be a part of that.

How is working with Ryan Coogler?

Ryan's a wonderful writer. I love collaborating with him and co-writing with him. When we work together, we'll write a half of the script and then flip it and rewrite each other. There is a lot of overlap. Oftentimes, we'll be sharing the document on a videocall and typing on the same document at the same time. It's a full-on collaborative process. It's not me writing it and then him tinkering what I do. He's a great writer and we just work together. Before working with Ryan, I had not written with someone, so now I'm super spoiled. It's fantastic.

Is there pressure on the sequel to a successful movie?

We constantly challenge each other with the characters to make them better, to make their actions feel grounded, to make their beliefs real, to have empathy with them, and put ourselves in their shoes, and have that drive their action as opposed to we need them to do "X" so we'll just have them do it. In terms of characterization, we take this approach whether it's a first movie, a sequel, the fourth movie, whatever: the pressure is the same. You put your head down and focus on telling a great story, and then you don't really have time to focus on the pressure. We all are aware of the success of the first movie. I personally am really, deeply appreciative to have been a part of it. But this movie has to stand on its own, and we all embraced that. We just move forward and do the work, and hold ourselves and each other accountable for doing the best we can and pouring ourselves, our whole heart, into the work.

FELLOW INVENTORS RIRI WILLIAMS
AND SHURI QUICKLY FORM A CLOSE BOND.

Executive, Production & Development at Marvel Studios, Nate Moore was present at the start of the *Black Panther* journey, with the first movie. He discusses the extraordinary ambition and creative challenge of the sequel.

NATE MOORE

PRODUCER

"We always knew there was something special to the first movie. We knew we had to dive back in."

Did you always feel that Black Panther *was a strong movie?*
We always knew there was something special to the first movie, but we also knew there was a risk. I remember going to San Diego Comic-Con [in July 2017] and playing the footage of the Busan car chase behind the cast to see how fired up both they and the audience would get. We were like, okay, there's an appetite here—if we do this right, people are going to love this movie. But it wasn't until opening weekend, when we saw the response from both the Black community and everybody worldwide, that we realized this was something really special. So we knew we had to dive back into the world of Wakanda and work out with Ryan Coogler what the sequel could be.

The new film comes from a place of tragedy.
The themes of tragedy and loss are inherent to Black Panther, even in *Captain America: Civil War.* In that film, T'Challa loses his father T'Chaka in a terrorist attack. So it is certainly something that this nation has dealt with through the centuries, I think, and it felt very much a part of the fabric of Wakanda to explore this theme again. Unfortunately, now there's a real-world context that we're dealing with. But narratively it didn't feel out of the box to come back to this theme and explore what it really means.

Are there parallels between how T'Challa and Shuri deal with grief in the two movies?
Absolutely. The scientist deals with death in a different way than the spiritualist does. Shuri throws herself into her scientific work as a way to avoid having to process that grief. T'Challa was more in touch with his spiritual side and with the traditions of Wakanda, so that, while the passing of T'Chaka was devastating to him, he was more emotionally equipped to deal with it. The people around Shuri respond to her in a much different way than they did with T'Challa. That's why Ramonda becomes such an important character. Here's a mother who has not only lost her husband but now her son, and whose daughter is dealing with grief. Ramonda is very much steeped in the traditions of Wakanda. There gets to be an interesting dichotomy of seeing these two women on a similar path and how their approach to that path accelerates or hinders their healing process.

This is more of a mother-daughter story.
It became immediately apparent to us that Shuri and Ramonda were the two central characters of the movie. They're dealing with the loss in the most personal way. We had already intimated that Ramonda had been ruling Wakanda in T'Challa's absence, so it made sense that Ramonda would continue to rule after the king's passing. She has her own point of view on the princess that inverts to some degree the dynamic between T'Chaka and T'Challa from the first film. T'Chaka was much more the diplomat, while T'Challa was the hothead. If anything, Ramonda is a bit more fiery here than Shuri, who is much cooler and laid-back. Ramonda's notion is to break Shuri out of her funk by making her uncomfortable. Shuri has been hiding in her lab since T'Challa's passing and Ramonda realizes that she needs to access the other part of Wakandan tradition in order to overcome this grief. To some degree, Ramonda sends Shuri on a mission, if for no other reason than to shake her out of her usual mind-set. The mission is the thing that ultimately starts to open Shuri up to the possibility of overcoming that grief.

How did Ryan Coogler approach the story?
Ryan is interested in the world and people, and he loves comics: Those things don't work in opposition to each other as they might with other filmmakers. When he was thinking about Namor and how to bring Namor's world to the screen, I don't think he was particularly interested in just doing the comic-accurate version; not because that's not interesting, but because there is a lack of specificity. As a filmmaker, he only really becomes invested in these characters when he understands where they come from. And there is, even as a fan of comics, a little bit of missing mythology in Namor's world, which Ryan wanted to fill in.

By planting Namor in a civilization that has a centuries-long history, Ryan was able to find something specific to those characters, which would resonate thematically with Wakanda. The notion of the typical Atlantis—as the world that sinks after a cataclysmic event—doesn't really have anything to do with the world of Wakanda or the themes of the first movie. But the notion of a society that was forced into hiding because of the events of the outside world—this is actually very much germane to the world of Black

THE NEW BLACK PANTHER SUIT FEATURES DISTINCTIVE
SILVER DOTS ON THE MASK, REFLECTING DOT PATTERNS
THAT SHURI PAINTS ON HER OWN FACE.

Panther in the MCU. Ryan is a very savvy filmmaker in putting these things together. He takes what is best about the comic publishing, but anchors it in a world context that people will understand. This breathes new life into ideas that otherwise might feel a little bit staid.

What are you most excited about for the movie?
This movie might be more ambitious than the first film from a technical standpoint and I do think it's going to entertain audiences in the way that Marvel movies like to entertain. But it also has a depth in how it deals with grief and shines a light on a society that often gets overlooked historically. There's such a rich history to the movie's costumes, and Ruth Carter, our costume designer, has upped her game in this film. She has brought even more looks into the world of Wakanda. I think outside of *Avengers: Endgame*, this might be the most challenging Marvel film to date. But that's part of why we're excited. Because there's so much potential to be so different than anything that has come before.

Played by Angela Bassett, Queen Ramonda is the widow of King T'Chaka and mother of King T'Challa. Let's learn more about the character, courtesy of the filmmakers.

QUEEN RAMONDA

QUEEN RAMONDA MAKES A STRIKING ENTRANCE
AT THE UN MEETING IN GENEVA.

DORA MILAJE WARRIOR OKOYE
WITH QUEEN RAMONDA.

Nate Moore (Producer):

It made sense to make Ramonda the new Queen of Wakanda. She'd been there when T'Chaka ruled, and when T'Challa ruled. We envisioned that during the five years between Marvel Studios' *Avengers: Infinity War* and *Endgame*, there needed to be almost a special election. We couldn't imagine someone not voting for Queen Ramonda at that point. She's such a powerful personality.

When we open the film, we see that Queen Ramonda is ruling well. She's respected. She makes decisions in a forthright way and listens to outside input. She's a really effective leader. But when Namor reveals himself, she has a big decision to make. Do I throw my lot in with this new, undefined radical agent? Or do I side with the surface world? As the film unfolds, Ramonda has a lot of things to juggle in order to figure out the best path forward for her country.

Ruth Carter (Costume Designer):

Every costume designer would want to adorn a queen. If you are given the task to dress the Queen of Wakanda, then it's a dream come true. Also, it being Angela Bassett, I can't think of a better scenario. Ryan really wanted Ramonda to enter the UN wearing a very regal outfit with a big, big presence. We brought in our 3-D artists to recreate the new crown that Ramonda wears at the UN. Her designs are all based on beauty, African royalty, and technology. Angela definitely empowers her costume.

Moore:

Ramonda is a woman who has been girded by loss; she has become a very, very successful queen of Wakanda and has done a great job in defending her nation from all comers. Yet her daughter is suffering from depression over the loss of her brother. It becomes Ramonda's job to try and pull Shuri out of this place and let her see that there is the potential to move forward through loss. It's a theme that hopefully people will really identify with because there's not one of us who hasn't had to deal with loss in some way or another. It's about becoming a hero in spite of that loss, not because of it.

Joe Robert Cole (Co-writer):

When T'Challa passed away, Shuri buried herself in

work in denial. Ramonda sees this and recognizes it; she's been through it. There's a ritual that Ramonda's tribe, the River Tribe, do to honor their connection to those who have passed. She comes to Shuri's lab and strong-arms her—in a sweet way—into going out to the bush for a couple of days, just the two of them together.

Moore:

Angela Bassett and Letitia Wright [Shuri] approach their craft in different ways. But the results are often very similar in that they deliver these really powerful performances. Each performance on its own would be enough to shape a movie, never mind having two of them. Angela is a pro. I mean, she is the consummate pro. She's able to deliver everything you want and adjust on the fly and is technically incredibly proficient. Letitia is a more intuitive actress who very much takes it from an inside place. She has to feel it first before she can do it. The conversations on set, oftentimes, are much different. But, again, the end result is two performances that are very true to the characters and deliver something that might be surprising to audiences.

Academy Award-nominated American actress Angela Bassett talked about her pivotal role as Queen Ramonda. Expect tales of Black pride, filming in Puerto Rico, and celebrating life, New Orleans-style.

ANGELA BASSETT
(QUEEN RAMONDA)

"Wakanda feels like it actually exists. It's just been so compelling and meant so very much to so many."

QUEEN RAMONDA WEARS GOLD AND PURPLE, SIGNIFYING HER STATUS AS WAKANDAN ROYALTY.

How was it to take on the role in Black Panther?

It was an offer that couldn't be refused; an opportunity to see women who look like me in their resplendent glory. Those opportunities were few and far between. A role quite like this had never quite been seen before. I have always been interested in African American history, and history in general. We've always been told, or we tell our kids, that you could be President or that we are descendants of kings and queens. Now, we have a moment where we can actually see that—it's make-believe, but audiences have embraced this. Wakanda feels like it actually exists. It's just been so compelling and meant so very much to so many.

Were you surprised by the global reaction?

I don't think I was surprised. Our African American culture and black culture has been at the forefront in art, fashion, music… It makes sense to me that this film would resonate in the way that it does. A decade or two ago it may have been surprising, but I wasn't surprised—though I was very, very pleased that it did as well as it did. Ryan has such a big heart and he is such a great storyteller. The actors that he's brought together, we're filled with emotion and passion. On set, we adore and appreciate one another. Our story originated in the comics, but the mother and daughter dynamic is real and universal. As artists, as individual actors, we embrace that.

What does it mean to you showing these films to your children?

It certainly has been very special. I was very, very proud to bring them to the premiere because it was a first. To see all this beautiful imagery and black royalty on screen—it was important to them, just like seeing the first African American President. It was a special time and a special film. It shattered so many preconceived notions. Expectations were realized and surpassed. So, I'm excited for them to see this movie as well.

How is Namor introduced in the movie?

It's been a year since the passing of Ramonda's son, Shuri's brother. Ramonda is steeped in tradition. She understands grieving, the various stages of it, with her husband and her son passing. Shuri is a young woman of science: it is not, presently, in Ramonda's nature to respect and embrace that, I think. But a mother knows. A mother can see. She has instincts. She takes her young daughter out to a certain place, and while they are there, security is breached. A stranger shows up out of nowhere: Namor. His nation has been hidden from the world, as Wakanda was—and he would like it to remain that way. Ramonda's most precious treasure is her daughter at this point. With Ramonda's husband and son gone, her embrace is that much tighter around Shuri, whereas Namor is just very much concerned with what he wants. There's a delicate dance between the two of them.

Are you impressed by the costumes?

I've worked with [Costume Designer] Ruth Carter a number of times and she is just absolutely brilliant. She received an Academy Award for her work on *Black Panther*. It's as if the first movie was grade school for her and, with this one, she has given us PhD graduate level. Ruth looks at every possibility in terms of her research and in connecting with other artists around the world to build the world of Wakanda—and not just Wakanda this time, but Mayan culture as well. To walk into the warehouse and see row after row after row, rack after rack, table after table of jewelry and materials and fabrics and costumes that she sourced from Africa, from around the world—it's just absolutely, absolutely amazing.

You did some shooting in Puerto Rico?

Puerto Rico is standing in for Nosy Nato in Madagascar, off the coast of Africa. This is where I meet Namor. I am to bring his shell and summon him. It was my first trip there—it's beautiful. The people are beautiful. I was really excited to be in this exotic location. I had to take a few swimming lessons. I thought I could swim a little bit, but, no—Olympic swimmers taught us how to breathe and hold our breath for free diving, that sort of thing. A few of us got really good at it. Me not being one of those people, I got good enough to do what I needed to do. I'm proud that I was able to accomplish that.

Ruth creates back-stories with her costumes.

She does. I know so much more about who I am playing when I put the costumes on. My costumes were a little simpler last time. But this time, the embroidery, the jewelry that's within the fabric, the capes, the headdress—Ruth really just took it up a notch. I felt so beautiful, so regal, in each and every costume. Ruth is magnificent, just as [Production Designer] Hannah Beachler is, too. When Shuri and I go on our retreat, where Namor emerges from the ocean, you would think in a movie like this there would be green screen. But, no, Hannah has really given us sand, earth, trees—and ships! There's so much detail. Also, our new director of photography, Autumn Durald: Maybe it's something about the strength of these women, so says the queen. They're excited to work with one another, and I think, I don't know, maybe that's what women do. Part of a family. Without ego—I think that's a huge part of it. Ryan must know something.

Tell us about working with Tenoch Huerta Mejìa (Namor).

Oh, I'm so excited for him, and he's so excited. I mean, just what this character and what it means for his people, for his nation, for the world. He comes prepared, and English is not his first language: respect to Tenoch. I've been happy to be on this journey with him, to be along with him, and to help him in whatever way that I can.

How did the loss of Chadwick affect you?

We were shocked. We didn't know [about his cancer] while it was happening. That would have brought up a different emotion in all of us, had we known what he was going through. And he would have none of that. He would have us do our best, I think, without that layer. Of course, when we came together to do this story, the presence of him was with us. The idea of him, the loss of him, the absence of him, you know, we all felt that and recognized that deeply. We can use this opportunity to honor him.

You found the celebration.

Yeah, that's a part of New Orleans culture, that we're able to embrace that. It's particular, I think, to just that little part of America. It gives lightness to our souls, lightness and joy to our sadness, which is a part of life.

ANGELA BASSETT WEARING ONE OF THE DISTINCTIVE DRESSES THAT COSTUME DESIGNER RUTH CARTER CREATED FOR HER CHARACTER.

T'Challa's talented younger sister Shuri is a scientific genius who, in the new film, is devastated by the unexpected loss of her brother. The filmmakers and cast discuss how they brought this challenging dynamic to the screen.

PRINCESS SHURI

Nate Moore (Producer):

For the story to move forward in a world where T'Challa is now no longer with us, it made sense to investigate what that loss meant for all of the people that he touched. And there's no one who's going to feel that effect more than his little sister, Shuri. Ryan thought it would be really interesting to explore how this woman had all the tools to invent anything she wants, but wasn't able to invent a cure for her brother's illness.

Joe Robert Cole (Co-writer):

In *Black Panther*, Shuri was the younger sister who could needle T'Challa. She was so witty, smart, and charming, and could stand toe to toe with him.

Moore:

Shuri is an innovator and the smartest person in the Wakanda. In the first film, she could give her big, older brother grief in a way that no one else can, which was a lot of fun. This movie requires a different tool set. But what's interesting about Letitia is that, even when we cast her, her dramatic chops were incredibly clear. Letitia was well equipped with that tool set going in, and it's been admirable in the way that she's tackled the performance. There is a reality to her performance.

Cole:

At the start of the film, Shuri is struggling with grief. How she responds to T'Challa's death tells you everything you need to know about how close they were. Ryan talked about the stages of grief and about how Shuri goes through that journey. Her relationship with her mother grows throughout the film.

Angela Bassett (Ramonda):

Working in scenes with Letitia, remembering where her character has come from, you see the tremendous growth and maturation, from being this science geek and this little sister.

Ryan Coogler (Writer and Director):

The loss of T'Challa has been devastating for Shuri. He has been there all her life and she wasn't expecting to lose him so young. In this, she's kind of an audience surrogate. It has been a year since he passed and Ramonda realizes that Shuri is still not healing. She suggests that they go on a retreat where they step away from the city and technology for a few days and perform a ritual. It is on this retreat that Namor shows up.

Ruth Carter (Costume Designer):

In the first film, we saw Shuri in bright colors. Now we see her in grays and more somber colors. We came up with some casual things for her to wear in the Wakandan bush and a track suit for when she goes to Boston. Through the storyline, her character starts to come to life. She doesn't stay in the somber mood that we first see her in. We also see a lot of her innovations, continuing a theme from the first film.

Moore:

When Namor brings the vibranium detector that he found to the shores of Wakanda, Shuri starts to pull it apart and she realizes that whoever made this is a genius—but in a completely different way than she is a genius. Shuri is a futurist, but this person is much more of an engineer. Her assumption is that the scientist is going to be Bruce Banner or Erik Selvig, or somebody in a high-tech extra-governmental body like DARPA or S.W.O.R.D. When she discovers that the scientist is actually a young woman named Riri Williams who goes to MIT, Shuri immediately feels a kinship with her.

MODERNITY AND TRADITION: MOTHER AND DAUGHTER
SHOW THEIR DIFFERENCES IN THEIR CLOTHES.

IN HER GRIEF OVER HER BROTHER'S
PASSING, SHURI THROWS HERSELF
INTO WORK IN HER LAB.

Guyanese-British actress Letitia Wright is excited to be reprising her role as Shuri. Here, she talks about the grieving process, the "cool dynamic" of her character meeting soul-mate Riri Williams—and sweet popcorn! Read on...

LETITIA WRIGHT
(PRINCESS SHURI)

"Shuri has to process grief unexpectedly. We see this young woman fight for purpose. This young woman is fighting for that drive every day."

How has Shuri changed in the new movie?
In *Black Panther*, Shuri is a breath of fresh air. She is so bold in her choices about science, technology, and creation. There's a space for Shuri to just be amazing, to make mistakes. She has her brother and her family. She has this lack of limitation. Her brother trusts her to create his whole Black Panther armor. We see this young woman in her element. Then she is transformed through the experience of loss and change. One of my favorite directors, Steve McQueen, said that sometimes life imitates art and sometimes art imitates life. When I read the script of the new film, it was this line that hit me, that art is imitating life. Shuri has to process grief unexpectedly. We see this young woman fight for purpose. We see this young woman fighting for that drive every day. Ryan wrote that beautifully.

Did you discuss how to play the grief with Angela?
Angela's been an amazing contribution to my life from the first film. She was always very caring and like a mother. I just love her so much. This film, it's just another extension of how she loves me as Letitia and how she loves me as my character, Shuri. We didn't really discuss it. It was just something that was felt in the room. Those words and those emotions and those scenes, we knew what was going on. In a sense, it was us holding each other's hands, processing together, and going through this with our characters.

How does the introduction of Namor affect things?
We are at a spiritual retreat, as I would call it. Ramonda's trying to allow Shuri to process and express how she's feeling about the loss of her brother. But Shuri's really in denial. She's like, hey, I've got this, I'm okay. She's processing in a way that's a bit closed off. So in this intimate moment where we think we're having some sort of breakthrough—pop, out comes Namor. It's freaky. He's popping out of the water. He's coming at us. And we're like, yo, what is this? We see Ramonda and Shuri transform from mother and daughter having a conversation to warrior mode. It's a beautiful way to interrupt the flow of what's going on with this family: We have to sidestep what's going on with our emotions and protect our nation. I think that's a great way to introduce Namor as someone that's just, you know, wrong timing, just absolutely wrong timing, but so powerful.

Were you surprised by the inclusion of Mayan culture?
It's beautiful that Namor and the Talokanil world and people are directly inspired by Mesoamerican history. We have a huge platform for this history to be celebrated, to be acknowledged by the world, maybe. This film allowed me to open up a textbook, you know, do my research and discover how wonderful this history is. It's beautiful to see the ways in which the different departments have come together to celebrate it: Ruth Carter, with costumes, with such detail, beauty, colors, and integrity; Hannah Beachler, our production designer, who doesn't miss a beat. It's beautiful to see them really go the extra mile and infuse the research into this film. The first film expressed the different colors and cultures within the African continent, and now they are combined with Mesoamerican culture. So, yeah, I'm feeling it. I think it's so dope.

AGAINST HER OWN FIRST INSTINCTS, SHURI TAKES ON THE MANTLE OF BLACK PANTHER.

It's bigger than entertainment.

Yeah, it's all about reaching and impacting. That's been the purpose of my whole career so far, to impact and reach people and let them know through my characters that they matter. If little kids, from a young age, are saying, I matter, I'm worth it, I'm worthy—that's amazing.

How does Shuri change in the film?

There's a coming-of-age moment where she's thinking that expressing her pain and her fury towards Namor through violence is going to be satisfying to her soul, and it's not. That's a beautiful way to develop her story arc. She realizes: wait, my brother wouldn't do this. She learns from that and becomes a woman. We see Shuri become a woman in her own right through this film.

How do you meet Riri Williams?

Namor wants us to find her. We don't know anything about this young girl, but when we come to America we find out that she's a super-smart scientist at MIT, this young black girl from Chicago just doing her own thing. She was able to build a machine that detects vibranium, which is meant to be undetectable. She's crushing it. We see these two amazing scientists just geek out about each other. Whoa, you're the princess of Wakanda. Whoa, you built this thing. It's so cool to see two young woman come together and champion each other, support each other, and protect each other. It's a cool dynamic.

How was shooting underwater?

That's funny because Ryan called me earlier last year and was like, hey, Tish, can you swim? I said, I thought my role was to be in my laboratory, what more do you need from me? So, I had to learn to swim very quickly.

ABOVE TOP: SHURI ON RIRI WILLIAMS' BIKE IN BOSTON.
ABOVE: SHURI WITH THE DORA MILAJE'S ANEKA.

QUEEN RAMONDA AND SHURI ARE INSTANTLY ON THEIR GUARD AT THEIR FIRST SIGHTING OF NAMOR.

They set up sessions and everybody was in their own little corner learning to swim, whether it's myself or Lupita or Danai or Winston. Everybody was learning to swim or perfecting their swimming, shall I say. Then we came to Atlanta and started the process of working with the underwater diving team, which was very cool. I learned to free-dive without an air tank.

What makes Ryan so amazing?

What makes Ryan Coogler an amazing human being to work with, and a great director, is his sensitivity. He is so sensitive and so caring. I am so honored that he's in my life. He has a great way of taking so much information and processing it and putting it in its place. He just wants the movie to be the best it can be. The way he expresses himself, the way he loves on everyone, and cares about each department and each thing that we have to do—it just comes out in the work. I fell in love with his directing on *Fruitvale Station* [Coogler's feature directorial debut in 2013]. I made a list of directors I wanted to work with. It was him, Steve McQueen [*12 Years a Slave*], Barry Jenkins [*Moonlight*, *If Beale Street Could Talk*]. I looked at that list a year after *Black Panther*, and I was like, "you're doing great, kid."

What aspects are you most excited about?

Oh, man, that is such a good question. I'm so excited about being able to tap into Wakanda again and seeing the world of Talokan. I'm excited about us honoring Chad. I'm excited for people to have joy and impact. I'm excited for the kids and the cosplay. I'm excited about a lot! I'm gonna be in the cinema with my IMAX glasses on… sweet popcorn—Americans like butter popcorn and salt: what is that about? Sweet popcorn, man. Just put some sweet on that. You gotta do it. Yeah.

BELOW: SHURI IN WAKANDA.
BELOW MIDDLE: TRANSFORMATION INTO BLACK PANTHER.
BOTTOM: SHURI IN A DEEP-SEA DIVING SUIT EXPLORES TALOKANIL.

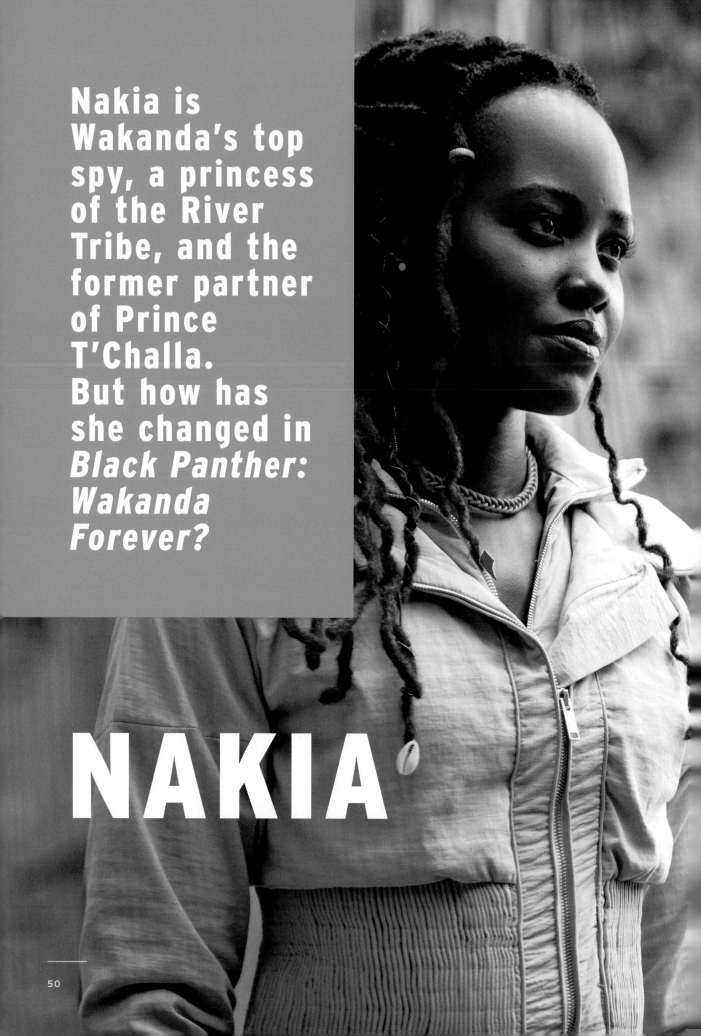

Nakia is Wakanda's top spy, a princess of the River Tribe, and the former partner of Prince T'Challa.
But how has she changed in *Black Panther: Wakanda Forever?*

NAKIA

Lupita Nyong'o (Nakia):

In the first film, Nakia is a lone wolf. She's idealistic and independent, and also has this incredible love relationship with T'Challa. Now, all these years later, after the big Blip and the loss of T'Challa, Nakia has matured. She entertains the word compromise more now, albeit still holding very strong, idealistic views. She has grown into a nurturing spirit, and is more organic and mellow.

Joe Robert Cole (Co-writer):

In *Black Panther*, Nakia was someone who was willing to break the rules, where Okoye, for instance, was more of a traditionalist. Okoye was at odds with Nakia at times. In this film, Okoye starts to take the journey away from being the staunch traditionalist we have known her to be throughout the films.

Nate Moore (Producer):

Black Panther: Wakanda Forever is about a family trying to readjust to a new normal. There are characters, like Nakia, Okoye, and M'Baku, who are very much entrenched in the family, even though they're not direct family members. But they're also having to deal with that same loss and figure out where they fit now in this new normal.

Nyong'o:

I love the array of costumes I wear in this film. Nakia is a spy, so I get to have fun and be other people. But my main costume is a diving suit that Ruth Carter created. I love being in it. It's got this metallic sheen to it, greens and blues. Working with Ruth is really fascinating because she's the calmest creator I know. She's creating these really intense costumes that are going to inform cosplay for a decade to come or more.

Ruth Carter (Costume Designer):

Nakia has a submersible suit that has a lot of bioluminescence to it. It has a lot of magic and tribal markings. We created the sketch for it, and it was decided very quickly that that would be the one that we would make. It took a lot of work to get those elements to lay right. There are some South African painters who do this wonderful full-body tattoo work that has tribal markings. That was one of the influences in creating Nakia's suit. We wanted to keep her in the green color, but also give her something that would reflect the beauty of the ocean and the bioluminescence. So we came up with foiling and paintwork in different levels of green— some bright, some blue, some lit up.

Lupita Nyong'o tells us about playing Nakia, and talks Black representation, female empowerment, and her intense underwater training regime for the film.

LUPITA NYONG'O

(NAKIA)

"There was an embracing of culture, of ethnicity, that went beyond that specific demographic that we were representing."

Were you surprised by the huge global success of the first movie?

The first *Black Panther* film is a testament to the power of specificity, being based on an African nation—fictitious, but an African nation no less. Africa was being celebrated rather than exploited, giving credit where credit was due: Black people were excited to see themselves. There was an embracing of culture, of ethnicity, that went beyond that specific demographic that we were representing. I mean, we had Korean people embracing the Korean clothes and Chinese people doing the same, and Mexican people as well. It was a reminder that we all come from very rich histories. In the second film, Ryan is going a step further by expanding the perspective. We're getting that Hispanic perspective in all its Mayan specificity. We're celebrating Mayan Hispanic culture, and I think this will resonate in an equal and new way for that demographic, when it sees itself front and center. It's like Wakanda really embracing Talokan, and the world having to just bathe in the majesty of these cultures.

How was the underwater work?

First of all, I have to say that Ryan seems to have something for water because even in the first film there were fights in the water. So, when I read this script, I was like, oh, he's really going into it this time. He's really embracing his fascination with water. Now, I've swum in a mediocre manner since I was little. Like, you know, I can float, but I panic swim. I used to swim like a puppy, you know what I mean? Not anything that anyone wants to film. I had to immediately get to training. I decided to go the extreme route. I did something called XPT Life [Extreme Performance Training], which was created by [big-wave surfer] Laird Hamilton and [his wife, ex-professional volleyball player], Gabrielle Reece. It involves breath work, movement underwater with weights, and incredible attention to restorative techniques like ice baths and saunas. It was amazing because it really opened my breath capacity. I could hold my breath for long periods of time in such a way that shooting became a lot easier. I also had an incredible swimming trainer, Pamela

Baldwin. She helped me make friends with the water. It's so easy to think that water is death. But, in order to be seamless with the water, you have to surrender to it. It's about allowing the water to receive you, instead of trying to stay up. It was a lot of fun.

How does it affect performance?

You have to be so present when you're dealing with water. There's no time for stage fright. You have to work against adrenaline. That's why the breath work is so important. You can't afford to hurry. You actually have to slow all the way down and focus, and you have to be able to pivot with the changes. And there's machinery under there when you're shooting, and so your mind has to be clear. You have to be present. And it was such a great lesson for performance in general. The most rewarding times on set for me are when I'm not worrying about how I'm looking. I'm not worrying about how I'm coming across. I'm just being and receiving what is coming my way. Underwater, there was no other alternative.

Does the icon of the Black Panther take a backseat now?

You know, the thing that sets Black Panther apart from all the other Super Heroes, as far as I know, is that he is the leader of a nation. His concerns are not self-serving: there is a psychology of the collective that is key to the Black Panther story line. So, Wakanda is Black Panther and Black Panther is Wakanda. For me, Wakanda is a symbol of home and of belonging. It's a symbol of community and how we hold on to each other to move forward. I think that's why everyone was able to relate to it, because everybody has a community. Also, the idea that other communities are threats or allies. These are things that we are talking about all the time in the world. Who are our people? Who do we align ourselves with? And what does it mean when that idea of alignment expands?

What's your take on Namor?

I love the way that Ryan's villains are never completely villainous. I remember when I read the first script, I kind of sided with Killmonger: His argument was persuasive, you know what I mean? Ryan's stories force us to contend with a moral and ethical battle, and that is very exciting. Namor is the leader of the Talokanil. He is in exactly the same position that Wakanda was in in our first film, where they have been living in secret all these years. They turn to Wakanda to solve the problem that Wakanda brought to their borders.

How did you feel being back on set?

It was really moving to come back to Wakanda and reunite with the cast. So much has happened in the last six years. We lost our sun—and I mean that, S-U-N, as well as S-O-N—in Chadwick. When it happened, the world had shut down, and everybody was isolated in their homes [due to the Covid-19 pandemic]. Some of us were able to go for his memorial service, but it was a time of deep disconnection. So to come back to this world that he was such a central part of without him was difficult, painful, but also really therapeutic. We were able to lean on each other and share our grief stories between takes. So, for us, this has been a very moving time, to come to terms with that loss, but also

to do it the way so many African peoples do it with a sense of celebration and continuation: a celebration of what Chadwick was able to achieve in his very short and meaningful life. I think we all continue to feel that a part of this movie is always going to be for him.

Does this movie feel like a celebration of female empowerment?

The first film established the DNA of feminism in Black Panther and in Wakanda, because the king was surrounded by influential and powerful females, who really informed how he made his decisions. I remember people really, really taking to that and kids being really inspired by Shuri's story, with the science and technology; Okoye, with her fearlessness as the head of the army; and Nakia, with her independence. So I think that this film is really the pivot to because of the unforeseen circumstance of losing Chadwick really allowed for a course we were already on. And so, yeah, the fact that now the core of our story is a mother-daughter story feels quite organic, actually.

ABOVE: NAKIA AND OKOYE HAVE CLOSE BONDS.
RIGHT: IN HAITI, WHERE NAKIA IS WORKING AS A TEACHER,
QUEEN RAMONDA ASKS FOR HELP.

Danai Gurira reprises her role as Okoye, the fierce leader of the Wakandan royal guard. We hear how she teams up with Shuri and meets a worthy foil in mighty Talokanil warrior, Attuma.

OKOYE

DANAI GURIRA AS OKOYE ON SET DURING THE FILMING OF THE CHASE SCENE IN BOSTON.

Ryan Coogler (Writer and Director):

Okoye is an incredible character. We knew she was going to be special when we were writing her and were delighted when Danai Gurira agreed to play her. We were thrilled with how audiences embraced the character and were really excited for her to come back in this film. She goes through a devastating series of events in this film.

Nate Moore (Producer):

It was really interesting to continue the evolution of Okoye. In in our minds, she is a traditionalist, a hard-liner about rules and preserving the culture of Wakanda at almost all costs. In this film, she finds those rules kind of bending back on her. She has to create her own identity out of the cloistered world of Wakanda for the first time. This forces her as a character to exercise new muscles and to make some decisions for the first time that are her own. I'm not saying she didn't have autonomy before, but she certainly was a product of a rules system that she liked to adhere to more often than not. Now, outside of that rule system, what does this character do when she has her own choices?

Coogler:

When Namor tells Shuri and Ramonda that he needs them to find the scientist who built the incredible vibranium detection machine, all he knows is that the scientist is from the US. Shuri and Ramonda have to go talk with Okoye and figure out whether Wakanda intelligence can find who this scientist is, but very quickly they realize that they can't.

Moore:

Part of the emotional journey for Okoye, who you could argue has never lost a fight, is that she is actually sent out into the world with Shuri to recover Riri Williams, the young scientist who actually built the vibranium detector. Okoye and Shuri don't have a ton of traction in the US, but they do have one ally: [CIA agent] Everett Ross from *Black Panther*. They go to Ross and ask for his help in finding this scientist, ostensibly to protect [the scientist], although they won't have made that decision quite yet.

Okoye's a powerful character in that she's charismatic without saying a lot. A lot of that is in Danai's stature and in her eyes. She's always watching. She's always very active in scenes even if she's not saying the most dialogue. In finding an Attuma, who ends up being a foil to Okoye through most of the film, we needed to find an actor who had a similar skill set, someone who wouldn't necessarily have a lot of dialogue, who had a physicality that was very obvious, who looked kind of iconic. For Alex Livinalli, whom we cast as Attuma, expressing that is almost harder for him because he's under a layer of blue prosthetics! But the great thing about Alex, and Attuma as a character, is while he is the heavy enforcer, if you will, he plays it with a smile. There's a little bit of charm there, a twinkle in the eye— he's having fun with the character. He's having fun even when he's fighting Okoye. So you get these two almost Samurai fighting each other: Okoye is all business and Attuma is a little bit playful. That's a fun color to play for a big character who otherwise could come off as frankly kind of just a big, dumb heavy, which wouldn't be interesting.

Wakanda's elite group of warriors, the Dora Milaje, were breakout stars of *Black Panther*. Here, filmmakers and cast reveal how the sequel gives the Dora an even greater role.

DORA MILAJE

GENERAL AYO WITH NEW ARMOR
IN *WAKANDA FOREVER*.

BELOW: AYO TAKES CONTROL.
BOTTOM: ANEKA (PLAYED BY MICHAELA COEL) WISHES LUCK
TO HER PARTNER, AYO.

Nate Moore (Producer):

The Dora Milaje are much-beloved characters. They made such an impression both in *Black Panther* and in the *Avengers* films that there was no question we had to continue their story. What we thought was interesting, though, was to kind of shake up their ranks.

Angela Barrett (Ramonda):

What Ryan has done in this movie is take different characters through different journeys, almost just flip them in a wonderful way. The story around the strength and empowerment of the female warrior has been a beautiful thing to see, especially now, when women's voices are so strong and unsilent. Okoye and the Dora Milaje have represented how beautiful that can be, with the shaved head, wearing red: the strength of that, which in Swahili is called *ase*, the power to make things happen. Okoye has made a sacrifice of her personal life for her country and has given her life in service to her queen, her king, her nation. And yet, even as strong as she is as a warrior, she is still fragile and frail and capable of making mistakes.

Moore:

When we first started building the Dora Milaje, I don't think we realized how much of a chord they would strike with audiences. Danai Gurira as Okoye, Florence Kasumba as Ayo—who was introduced in Marvel Studios' *Captain America: Civil War* before Okoye—and the Dora in general were characters whom we loved. But you always want to see how audiences react before you make a determination as to where they could go. And, obviously, when *Black Panther* came out, they hit in a big way. So, we had these new characters that we could use both in giant movies like *Avengers: Infinity War* and *Avengers: Endgame*, but also use in smaller ways, such as when Florence Kasumba's Ayo showed up in *The Falcon and The Winter Soldier*. They're interesting enough characters that they allow you to do a lot of different things and they're iconic enough that audiences have a really visceral reaction when they see them.

Ruth Carter (Costume Designer):

The Dora Milaje wear completely new shoulder armor, but Okoye wears the original armor. She is the purist, a traditionalist. When you see her in the film, she does not

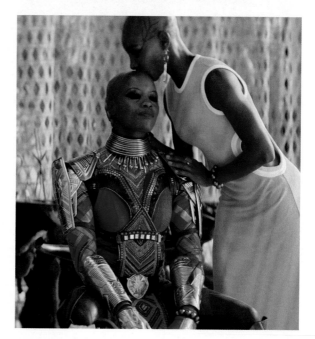

have the upgraded armor. She does not have anything new to her suit. It is as it was in *Black Panther*. Ryan Coogler made this story choice. We're building a story around the culture that we built in the first film.

Moore:

The Dora Milaje are at the forefront of protecting Wakanda. These incredibly capable fighters now find themselves out in the field defending vibranium and Wakandan technology from the rest of the world, out of necessity, but also because of the absence of the Black Panther. Wakanda's protector is no longer there to stop people from trying to take vibranium.

Making her first comic-book appearance in 2016's *Invincible Iron Man* #6, Riri Williams is a 15-year old engineer from Chicago who builds her own Iron Man-style armored suit.

RIRI WILLIAMS

Ryan Coogler (Writer and Director):
We decided early on to bring in Riri Williams, even before Chad passed away. In the early screenplay, once Shuri and Okoye got to the US and had to figure out what was going on with this [vibranium locating] machine, we knew Riri would be involved.

Nate Moore (Producer):
Riri Williams was the perfect character to slot in, for a number of reasons. She figures out how to find vibranium in the oceans, which makes Namor target her. Shuri also sees herself reflected in Riri in a contemporary and a surprising way. In the comics, Riri is so compelling. She lost her stepfather and her best friend in a tragic way, so there is this idea of shared grief [with Shuri], of shared trauma. These two women are trying to figure their way out of this sense of trauma, and being able to explore this theme helps to anchor Riri in the story on more than just a plot level.

Ruth Carter (Costume Designer):
We're introduced to Riri doing exams for other students for money. She's very much an MIT tech student, but she's also a gear head who has helped her dad build car engines.

Moore:
When Shuri finds Riri, she finds a version of herself who grew up in the US. Riri is smart, funny, and innovative. In some ways, she doesn't realize how smart she really is. Shuri has been celebrated for her intelligence in Wakanda, but Riri has been kind of discounted because of what she looks like, even at MIT, where everybody is probably the smartest person you or I will ever meet. So it is really interesting to see Shuri and Riri interact with each other, where these two very smart women realize both the similarities and the difference they have with each other.

Coogler:
Riri's an extremely talented mechanical engineer and works with her hands a little differently from Shuri, who has a staff. Actually, Shuri is proficient in a very wide array of disciplines: She has very deep knowledge of a lot of stuff, from biomedicine to aeronautics to artificial intelligence. Shuri is in on all of it. Riri has a very, very strict focus, but she's probably the best person alive at

building machines, robots, and things that can go fast. When we meet her, she's working out of a lab that's also an auto body shop, and we discover that she used to work on cars with her stepdad. She builds things like big combustion engines. So it's a different vibe from Shuri. Riri gets her hands dirty, she gets in there with a wrench and steel, and she's doing rivets.

Moore:
It's also really fun to bring Riri Williams into Wakanda and see what she thinks of this magical world. Up to that point, it's really only the Avengers and Everett Ross who had ever been in Wakanda. But never before had an African American girl come into this place and gotten a sense of the possibilities, the possibilities of technology, the possibilities of ownership of that technology. There's a lot of great drama, humor, and fun to be had with Riri Williams as a part of this ensemble cast.

Coogler:
The biggest thing that excites me about bringing in Riri is that from Shuri's perspective she sees a lot of herself in Riri. Shuri makes some decisions to look after her, even though Riri doesn't feel like she's a person who needs looking after. Shuri has a little bit of wisdom there and a lot of empathy for her. They form a connection, but it sets Wakanda and Talokan off on a very intense path.

Moore:
Dominique Thorne actually auditioned for the role of Shuri in the first movie. We really liked her and thought she was really smart. She has a great presence and is funny, with a lot of attitude. When we decided to put Riri Williams into *Black Panther: Wakanda Forever*, Dominique was our first and only call. We remembered her earlier audition, so it was very easy for Ryan, Sarah Finn [casting director], Kevin Feige [president of Marvel Studios], and the whole team to embrace the idea. We called her out of the blue. She hadn't heard from us in two-plus years. We offered her the role and she was game. She is such a talented actress who can play both drama and comedy. She's incredibly prepared and game for all the physical stuff that these movies tend to throw at performers, which can be, at times, really surprising. We're really excited both to tell her story here and in [the upcoming Disney+ series] *Ironheart*.

Riri Williams's Prototype Ironheart Suit is powered by thrusters and equipped with repulsor weapons. Let's discover the secrets of the construction of this scene-stealing movie costume.

IRONHEART SUIT

Ruth Carter (Costume Designer):
Riri Williams builds a suit, called the Ironheart suit, that really impresses Shuri—it flies, shoots, and does all kinds of things. When you're talking about that many gadgets and a costume that's purely based on technology, you need to create with a team. A Marvel Studios team brought all of the gadgets together, with a story of what they would do.

Ryan Coogler (Writer and Director):
Riri's Ironheart suit looks a lot different from the stuff you saw Tony Stark run around in. When you see the machines that she's building, it blows your mind a bit.

Carter:
It's a very difficult costume to craft. It's actually put together through some mold work, but also there's metalwork that we had made at [practical special effects studio] Legacy Effects in Los Angeles. It's made of all kinds of mechanical parts. We looked at a lot of illustrations that came out of VisDev [the Visual Development team at Marvel Studios]. We had meetings to discuss what what the cannons do, what her arm pieces do, how she moves about. Does she have a joystick that helps her turn and twist? So many elements to the Ironheart suit had to be sussed out. We dealt with it as its own separate body of intel and of build and craft.

There were a lot of discussions about how closely it would relate to the Iron Man costume. Ryan wanted it to be red, and we moved the heart to the side. Legacy Effects went to work doing the same thing, but only half of the costume was actually built. We built a maquette of the full suit, which they are able to use with visual effects. When Dominique came to set, she basically was in football pads. Movie magic went on with that costume, because it had to perform such fantastical things in the air, like spinning and diving—all kinds of stuff that she would not have been able to do in a full costume.

ABOVE: RIRI IN HER WORKSHOP AND TESTING OUT THE SUIT.

RIRI WILLIAMS ENCASED IN THE IRONHEART SUIT.

LIKE SHURI, RIRI WILLIAMS IS A TECH FIEND WHO LIKES
TO TINKER—IN A BIG WAY!

M'Baku, played by Tobagonian actor Winston Duke, is the leader of the Jabari Tribe on Wakanda. Here, the filmmakers reveal how he's changed from the first film to this one.

M'BAKU

Nate Moore (Producer):
Winston Duke is back as M'Baku and he is bigger and better than ever. M'Baku is a character who, in the first film, came down from the mountain, if you will, and participated in Wakanda in a way that he and his tribe, the Jabari, hadn't in the past. When we find him in this film, he is now a full participant in the Wakandan government and has opinions that are very much his own. He finds himself initially at odds with some of the decisions that Ramonda and Shuri are making. So M'Baku and the Jabari are much more active members this time around in what's happening. We get to see them fully integrated for the first time, which is really interesting.

Ryan Coogler (Writer and Director):
Even though it's a monarchy, Wakanda is still run in a democratic way with a lot of internal politics. We see Ramonda dealing with conflict and disappointment, whether it's Shuri, Okoye, or other characters. Everybody has a perspective: M'Baku is a part of the council now, after the events of the first film, so he has a view on the country as a whole. But he's still Jabari to the core and he fights to have as much power as possible. He wants the Jabari Tribe's voices to be heard and for the decisions that Wakanda makes to have a positive effect on the Jabari.

Moore:
Initially, the tribal elders support Ramonda's proposal to help Namor find the American scientist who built the vibranium-locating machine. They understand the potential threat that Namor poses. But one person opposes this plan and that's M'Baku. M'Baku and the Jabari believe that if Ramonda agrees to do this, she could be opening the door for Namor to come with another ask. M'Baku's concern is that Wakanda will become Namor's errand boy, or whipping boy, which he thinks is a strategic problem.

Joe Robert Cole (Co-writer):
M'Baku has a pretty awesome arc in the film. He goes from wanting to kill Namor—saying, let's go find him and kill him. But in the end, he comes to see that Namor is a god to his people, so if the Wakandans kill him, they will be at war forever, so they shouldn't do it. M'Baku ultimately ends up in a very unlikely place at the end of the film.

Moore:
For the first time, M'Baku as a ruler is really having to weigh what's best for Jabari land and for Wakanda as a whole. M'Baku is someone who doesn't particularly care for the outside world, but, for the first time, he is having to weigh the value of human life beyond the borders of Wakanda. That's an interesting place to put this character.

ABOVE TOP: M'BAKU IN A SCENE WITH SHURI.
ABOVE: M'BAKU IN HIS JABARI ARMOR.

The filmmakers share their perspectives on the movie's antagonist, Namor, and the degree to which he conforms to, and differs from, his comic-book counterpart.

NAMOR

Joe Robert Cole (Co-writer):
While we were writing the first movie, we talked about Namor being in Marvel Studios' *Black Panther: Wakanda Forever*. In the comics, Namor and T'Challa have a great rivalry and so we knew he could be a great foil.

Nate Moore (Producer):
Namor and Atlantis are some of the oldest characters in Marvel publishing. But for us to introduce Namor into the MCU, there needed to be something that really grounded him in a reality that felt as tactile as the world of Wakanda. In talking with Ryan and figuring out how to bring this character to life, one thing we thought was really interesting was viewing Namor through the lens of Mesoamerican culture, and specifically the Mayan Empire in the sixteenth century, during the Spanish colonization of the Americas. In our story, Namor leads an offshoot of a group of Mayans who, in an effort to escape the Spanish, find a magical flower that grows in water; what they don't realize is that the flower is vibranium-enriched. Ingesting the flower gives this small pocket of Mayan civilization the ability to breathe underwater. But unfortunately it takes away their ability to breathe on land, so Namor's people are forced to flee underwater and build a new city: Talokan.

Moore:
Namor sees the surface world through the lens of colonization, since his people, the Mayans, were conquered by the Spanish conquistadores in their search for rubber, cocoa, and other goods. When Namor realizes that the surface world now knows there's vibranium in the oceans, he sees this as a cycle that could repeat itself. His instinct is to strike first and strike hard. Wakanda finds itself protecting the surface world from Namor: They see his point but cannot accept the amount of blood he's willing to shed in order to protect his people.

Moore:
Namor is pretty comic-book accurate. He has the ankle wings and doesn't wear much clothing—it wouldn't make sense for him to have a huge robe or anything too elaborate because he's swimming underwater.

Cole:
He ages slower. He's incredibly strong. He can breathe both underwater and out of water. The wings on his ankles allow him the gift of flight. Namor has become the king of Talokan and in some respects is almost seen as a godlike figure because of the slowness by which he ages.

Moore:
We wanted to take the silhouettes from the comic books and breathe new life into them so that, for fans, they still see how we got from A to C. The designs for Namor tend to be pretty simple. We all know the green swimsuit, the trident, the ears, and the wings.

Ruth Carter (Costume Designer):
Namor wears these bathing trunks that came from the comics—we kept them, even though the Mayans wore loincloths and wraps. We took those shorts and we beaded them; we added little touches to connect him to his people, but we kept it pure with what he looked like in the comics.

Moore:
Tenoch Huerta Mejìa, who plays Namor, is an incredibly talented actor who was in [Netflix's] *Narcos: Mexico*, among other things. We were looking for someone who could embody Namor and elevate him above his arrogant, holier-than-thou comic persona. Here is a man who believes 100 percent that he is the hero in his own story. Namor doesn't see himself as a villain. He's not interested in ruling the world for power. He's not interested in money. He's interested in protecting his people.

Ryan Coogler (Writer and Director):
Namor has lived a really long time and knows no equal in terms of his capabilities. He can fly and breathe both underwater and at high altitudes. This guy doesn't need to put a lot of clothes on when he comes out of the water. He just comes out, says what he needs to say, and goes right back into the water, where he wants to be!

Moore:
Namor puts himself into conflict with Wakanda because he seems to be targeting an innocent bystander: Riri Williams. Tenoch's performance is really interesting because he's seductive and he's smart, with a soulfulness in his eyes. He is passionate about what he believes in and at certain points in the movie, he begins winning over our heroes. It's only because of the extremity of his actions that he is the antagonist for the film.

It's time to meet Mexican actor, Tenoch Huerta Mejìa, who plays Namor, King of the Talokanil. Let's hear about his experience of playing a Marvel Super Hero for the first time– and how he feels as if he's acting in his pajamas!

TENOCH HUERTA MEJÌA

(NAMOR)

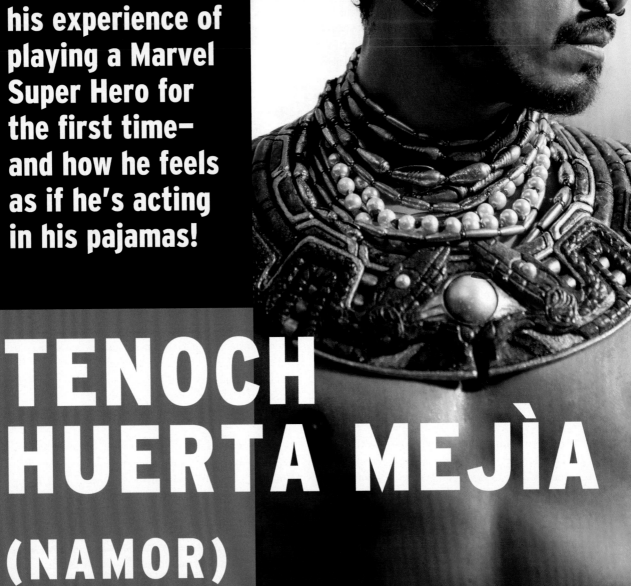

"It's a fantastic opportunity because Ryan is the right director for the right movie."

Can you believe you're playing one of Marvel Comics' first-ever Super Heroes?

Yeah, it's a dream. I've never imagined to be here playing this character—who is really important and one of the first Super Heroes. How they created the base of the character, with Mayan culture, is amazing. They made a really good job, not just with the story, but with the sets and every element onscreen, which are all based on original artifacts and artworks from Mayan culture. For me, of course, I'm Mexican—I hope this character is going to be really important in terms of representation for many, many kids all around the world, especially in Latin America. And, by the way, this is the first movie that my daughter can see because I usually make dramas [like *Narcos: Mexico*] in which everybody's dying, having big troubles, and whatever. But this is the first movie where my daughter can go to the premiere!

You're going to be your daughter's Super Hero.

Yeah, yeah. I just hope to have some respect from her when she is a teenager. I'm going to say to her, I'm a Super Hero—come on, shut up!

Are you proficient in Mayan now?

Josue, our Mayan dialect coach, was fantastic. He's Mayan, descended from the ancient Mayans. Josue talked with us all the time. We took classes—and I'm the worst, I have to say. I'm the worst in Mayan. I'm the last in my class! Guilty. But Josue explained the meaning of the words and phrases, how to articulate not just the words but the emotions. In the end you understand that we are exactly the same; there isn't any difference between an American, a Mexican, a Mayan, a Spaniard, or a German. We are human beings. Of course, we have differences. We have language. We have culture. We have a lot of things. But in the end, when you see through all those superficial aspects, we are the same.

Tell us about working with Ryan Coogler

It's a fantastic opportunity because he's the right director for the right movie. He has the sensibility and knowledge: as a genius, as a director, he's fantastic. If you discover something in the middle of the scene, you can say to him, I discovered this. This may affect the whole narrative, but he's totally open to it. He will say, yeah, let's change it. Let's make these adjustments to create a better and more accurate world in this movie.

Did you have to do training?

Yeah. But—funny story—when Ryan called me the first time to offer me this character, we had a videocall. He said, we are going to make this movie, it's about a Mayan Super Hero, the story is this shaman gives them a potion and they jump into the sea—and then my screen froze. When the screen started working again, I heard him say "…and that's it. What do you think?" I was like, yeah, yeah, I'm in. Then he asked me whether I knew how to swim. I said, I've never drowned before. He was, oh,

ABOVE: TENOCH ON SET IN FRONT OF BLUE SCREEN.
LEFT: FILMING WATER SCENES IN FLORIDA.

that's a good joke, and that was it. I told my agent I thought they were offering me the part of a shaman or something like that. Then Nate [Moore, Producer] called me and asked me if I knew how to swim. I hadn't realized they wanted me to play Namor! I didn't realize it was for real—and I really didn't know how to swim!

Was the training crazy?
I took swimming classes in Mexico. The thing that I love the most is free diving. It is so fantastic and peaceful. When you are down in the tank, everything is silent; it's like active meditation, in a way. I can hold my breath for five minutes. That's my record. Of course, Mabel [Cadena, Namora] can kick my ass. She can hold eight minutes. Eight minutes in her first try. Everybody was like, what? Eight minutes? After one month, I could hold my breath for five minutes. After one month! She's a Super Hero. She's the real Super Hero here.

Tell us about the costume.
You know, I feel like I'm acting in my pajamas because that's how I sleep, with just my shorts on. I had to go on a strict diet so I could fit those shorts and look fantastic, or try to look fantastic. But, yes, the costumes are fantastic. Every one of them, even the simplest of the costumes, is amazing, all of them. They make your job as an actor easier, you know what I mean? Because you are not pretending to look cool. You do look cool. You just need to wear the costume and do your job. I like it!

Is it hard to act wearing the helmet?
It's like you need a crane to be in position! No, but it's great. I love it. When I saw the helmet for first time, I immediately began to imagine how I would look wearing it.

I can imagine the action figure with the helmet and the wings! It's great—I can fly, I can swim, I'm strong, I'm even smart. My character is smarter than me, which is great!

How does the film honor Chadwick?
I think the fact that they never tried to re-cast the character, that's really important. To keep going and make a movie, it's the best way to say thank you, you know? From my perspective, the best way to say thank you when somebody gives you something is to wear it: wear the shirt, wear the pants, eat the cake, or whatever people give you. So, to make the next movie and integrate what happened in real life, it's the best way to say thank you, buddy. And on a personal level, what this movie means for me and for millions of brown- and black-skinned people in Latin America is great.

ABOVE TOP: NAMOR WITH JADE ADORNMENTS.
ABOVE (LEFT TO RIGHT): FILMING A WATER SCENE; WITH NAMORA
AND TALOKANIL WARRIOR; HEAD-TO-HEAD WITH NAMORA.

Namor's cousin, Namora, played by Mexican actress Mabel Cadena, is Talokanil royalty and a kick-ass warrior. Let's learn more about her from the filmmakers and cast.

NAMORA

Nate Moore (Producer):

Mabel Cadena's Namora, I think, may be the breakout character. She has such a fantastic face and a great physicality, and she's probably the most athletic cast member we have. So, we could do a lot with her. But what's great about Namor, Attuma, and Namora is there is a dynamic there. Even though we're not seeing the full breadth of their relationships, there is an interpersonal dynamic there that I think audiences will take away from the film. Mabel's incredibly talented. She's really funny. At times, she is the most dangerous woman on set. So we're really excited for people to see her in action.

Tenoch Huerta Mejìa (Namor):

Namora is smart and really brave. She is fantastic, you know? But she's young compared to Namor. He's five hundred years old or so. So, for him, it's like, okay, she's brave, because she's young. She's powerful, like an explosion. Namor is more like, the fight is not an explosion. It's little by little. He's more in control, so he's trying to guide her, but at the same time she is his right arm. I think Namor, as a character, has a lot of potential.

Ruth Carter (Costume Designer):

Namora is our new female character in this world, and she is just such a strong power player, a powerhouse warrior. Her headpiece was based on the lionfish. It's huge, massive. We created her costumes for regular life in Talokan, because Ryan wanted to show Talokan as a peaceful world that was not always fighting and at war. We came up with these fabrics and dyes to create ombré [color blended] effects and created this water story within the color palette of her costumes. She became part of the MCU world, but also very unique to the Talokanil world: We used fabrics that were sometimes very floaty and sheer and had a lot of beauty to them. I felt that her costumes throughout, across the board, were very unique and successful.

Huerta:

Mabel is one of the best Mexican actresses now. Before I met her, I watched some of her movies. For me, it was like, oh my God, who is this girl? I think when they chose Mabel, they made the best and the most right choose that they could make for this movie and in the future. I admire her and I feel blessed to work with her, to share this journey with her, to be both of us in this world for the first time in our careers. I think it's capital to have good allies when you are in a new world.

Venezuelan American actor Alex Livinalli, who plays Talokanil warrior Attuma, talks about water training, learning Mayan, being painted blue–and talking baseball with Ryan Coogler.

ALEX LIVINALLI

(ATTUMA)

"Attuma is a fighter, but also just a very lovable person."

ATTUMA STANDS READY FOR HIS FIRST FACE-TO-FACE BATTLE WITH THE WAKANDANS.

What was your reaction to joining the MCU on a **Black Panther** *movie?*

It was very surreal. I remember getting the call and it was just a multitude of emotions: excitement and feeling somewhat scared, a lot of things that I can't explain. Like, am I being punked? You know, that kind of thing. Then after I settle in, of course, I call my mother and then, you know, I cry. I was like, Mom, I'm in the MCU. So, it was a very special moment.

It's a very special company of actors.

It is. It's very exciting. The Black Panther itself is such a symbol, not only for the African American community. But me, being Hispanic, I see it as a symbol of hope. I'm excited to see how young kids who came over here from South America or Central America will see it—hey, there's someone that looks like me up there. There's someone that came over here as a child from South America and just made something out of himself.

Introduce us to Attuma.

When I got the job I immediately went online and started searching for this guy. I mean, I had no idea who Attuma was, or Namor, or any of those people. I was like, wow, this guy's a bad, bad, bad man. Then I had a meeting with Ryan and he explained that what we're doing is very different than what we've seen in the comic books. So that was very special because when I got to know this guy—when I read the script and understood the relationship he has with Namor and Namora—yes, he's a fighter, but the way I see him, he's just a very loveable person. He has love for his people, love for Namor, love for Namora, love for his way of life, which he's willing to protect, like a father protecting his family. That's who Attuma is: If you compromise my way of life, you're gonna see how much I love fighting as well, kinda thing.

His motivations are clear and commendable.

The main thing that I love about the story is that there's not like a clear bad person, like a clear antagonist. It's just like we're fighting for our way of life. You know, we don't want to be exposed to the world where they can come and take our things or make our life different. So we're fighting for our people not because we just want to fight, because we want to take someone's something. Just preserving our way of life, that's what we're doing.

How was the training?

I did a lot of working out and a lot of eating. I was eating every ten seconds, consuming about 6,000 calories a day, and I gained 30 pounds. I really wanted to make Attuma just bigger than everybody else, physically, to create that intimidating size. There was also a lot of water training. On my first day, I could only only hold my breath underwater for 30 seconds. But then, throughout the work, I ended up just going down there and just staying there for like three minutes, three and a half minutes. It was so much fun being in the tank: like, I can swim, but I was able to learn how to dolphin kick. That was very fun and exciting. We would play games where the safety team would place sandbags in the water, like an obstacle course. Then you would go down in one breath and walk towards a sandbag, pick it up, and then walk towards the other one, go to the end, and then come back. It took me quite a few weeks to actually go the distance. But once I did it, man, it was so satisfying.

Tell us about the blue look.

When we started filming, it would take about four hours. But as time went on, we compressed that into two and a half. The Talokanil cannot breathe outside of the water. So we use a breathing mask with liquid inside and we breathe through the liquid. As we get closer to the light outside the water, our skin turns blue in a protective way. It's a layer of blue paint covered with gold, green, and other shades of blue. There are different layers to it. The makeup team is just amazing at the stuff they do.

What kind of research went into the role?

Josue, our coach, is 100 percent Mayan, from Campeche [a state in southeast Mexico]. We've been working on the language since the beginning—and it's not an easy language. I've learned some Comanche and Lakota [languages spoken by Native American peoples] and I find them easier to speak than Mayan. There's a musicality to it, though it's very different than Spanish. Early on, I thought there's got to be some Spanish in it. But, *nada*. Josue did such a great job in the translation, explaining what individual words mean. You're able to be more expressive when you know the exact definition of each word, not just the entire phrase.

What was it like, working with Ryan?

The experience of working with him has been amazing. From the very first moment that we had our meeting, which was a videocall, we didn't really talk about Attuma. It was more like, tell me about you. Tell me about your life experiences. What do you like to do? Did you play any sports? What was school like? Where are you from? What do you eat? That kind of thing. That conversation transformed into what we do on set because that's how he communicated with me. I'm a big basketball fan, and so is Ryan. So, a lot of our conversations about the character and the scene transcended into, all right, in this scene, you know, you just won the championship, kind of thing—I felt that this communication was very special to me.

How about working with Danai [Gurira, Okoye]?

I was intimidated. I'm not going to lie. I've seen Danai on TV for years in *The Walking Dead*. But she's been great. I worked with her the most, and she's been the most amazing person in the sense of—this is my first time in the MCU, and doing something this big. She just held by my hand and walked me through everything. Every question that I had, she was there. Every take, all right, what do you need? She was very open to working with me. I'm just grateful for that. Also, she spoke to me in Mayan: She gives me these lines, like "Hey, Warrior!" You get goose bumps, seeing these two cultures, these two fighters.

"This is a water movie through and through." So says Director Ryan Coogler, and here the filmmakers dive into some of the secrets of how they brought this underwater world to life.

FILMING UNDER-WATER

Nate Moore (Producer):

When we decided to do the story of Namor and the Talokan, we knew there would be a huge water element in the movie. It's unavoidable. We built four or five separate water tanks in Atlanta to capture wet for wet photography, in addition to doing the dry for wet work ["wet for wet" is the term used for filming in actual water, while "dry for wet" refers to filming on a dry stage with practical and special effects used to simulate a character being underwater]. Both of those techniques give you different things, but there is something really special about underwater photography that you can't mimic.

Ryan Coogler (Director):

We built an outdoor tank that was 30 feet by 60 feet, and 14 feet deep at some points. It was right there in the parking lot at OFS [the 160-acre movie studio campus in Atlanta], where we shot a lot of the outdoor scenes in the first *Black Panther* film, including Warrior Falls. I learned how to swim a few years ago specifically for this movie. They had it set up for me to direct from the water in a scuba suit—though I was out of the water most of the time!

Alex Livinalli (Attuma):

If I hadn't had the training in the water tank, I don't think I could've done the dry for wet realistically. We spent so much time in the water that just feeling the motion of floating or being neutral, or using your hands to turn. Everything's very majestic in a way, the way that you move underwater.

Moore:

The way that people move in water tends to be more real than when they're out of water. What's interesting about Namor and the Talokanil is they're actually kind of super soldiers in water. They're going to want to move through water in a way that the human body probably can't. So there needs to be an interesting marriage between the stuff that we shoot underwater wet for wet and some of the stuff we shoot out of water dry for wet because the Talokanil are frankly stronger and faster swimmers than any human on the planet.

Coogler:

Our director of photography, Autumn Durald, prepped all kinds of different rigs and setups for filming underwater, and our visual effects team worked with our stunt folks and underwater photography team to achieve some of the different looks seen in the film. In the scenes where Wakandans are underwater, we used wet for wet. The actors just held their breath underwater! But the Talokanil have gills and their interactions with water are totally different than what any human actor's interactions would be. We had to find ways to achieve that. We looked at what had been done on other films and found some new approaches, which was exciting—and daunting!

Moore:

Water tends to be a very difficult thing to shoot and that was a real challenge for Autumn and everybody on the camera team. Stunt coordinators Andy Gill and Chris Dennison and visual effects supervisor Geoff Baumann and visual effects producer Nicole Rowley had to figure out the different ways that Wakandans might move through water versus the Talokanil. Math and geometry was done constantly to make sure that those two different groups of people were moving differently. There is an internal logic to how everybody moves.

Ruth Carter (Costume Designer):

It's a bit of a thing to understand what the camera is going to see, especially underwater. We had a big, twenty-foot tank on Stage 7. Everybody wanted to jump into the tank and just swim around, but we wanted to put our costumes on camera and see just how dark it was underwater with the lighting: how luminescent everything would be, how impactful. There were costumes that actually didn't make the movie because once we got them in the water, we just thought that they didn't make enough of a statement or didn't serve the story.

ABOVE LEFT: SHURI AND NAMOR IN THE DEPTHS.
ABOVE RIGHT: COSTUMES WERE SPECIALLY DESIGNED FOR UNDERWATER FILMING.

THE TALOKANIL RIDE ON THEIR DEEP-SEA TRANSPORTS: ORCA, OR KILLER, WHALES. ART BY PHIL BOUTTÉ.

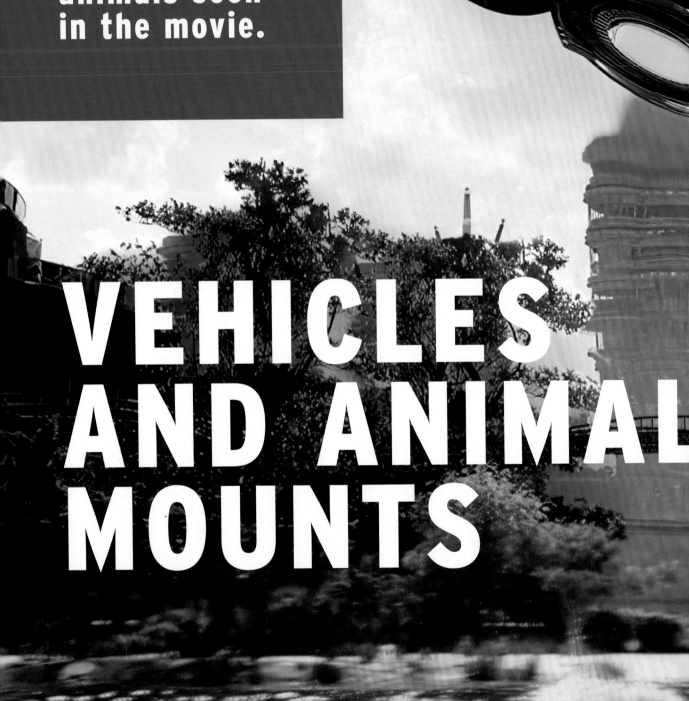

The filmmakers and some of the cast discuss the incredible array of new vehicles and marine animals seen in the movie.

VEHICLES AND ANIMAL MOUNTS

Ryan Coogler (Director):
We've got some really incredible ocean animals in there: whales and orcas. We've got some blue whales in there, and a lot of ocean mammals that the Talokanil have relationships with, similar to how people interact with horses or dogs. The whales kind of register on an even higher intelligence level, so we'll see them doing some really, really cool stuff in the battles.

Nate Moore (Producer):
The world of Talokan is really interesting because, much like the Mayan world on the surface at the time, it's agriculturally based: The Talokanil use beasts of burden and have figured out how to train underwater animals to help them. However, they don't armor their underwater animals and they don't build vehicles because they don't need them. They travel so fast themselves or by riding orcas and whales that they don't need traditional vehicles.

Joe Robert (Screenwriter):
We tried to figure out a new way for the Talokanil to interact with and ride orcas. They're like horses in some regards, but they don't ride them by straddling them. They're not everywhere, either; they're around, but they're not everywhere. It's not a heavy, heavy marine animal movie, but they do exist. We use them at in some really impactful and cool moments, where we allow them to really shine.

Alex Livinalli (Attuma):
The Talokanil ride whales, which is mind-blowing. When I read it in the script, I thought it would probably be greenscreen and we would be on top of some padding. But there's an actual whale—you just feel like a little kid. It's like, oh, I want to jump on that! You try to associate it with something that you're familiar with, like riding a horse. For the Talokanil, riding sea creatures is just everyday life. They live among whales, so they use them for traveling.

Ryan Coogler:
The Talokanil use hydro bombs: these devices actually create water through a chemical reaction with the molecules in the air. Then all of a sudden, you've got a lake's worth of water inside a building! The Wakandans are not really sure how to react to that kind of stuff.

Nate Moore:

As well as the underwater world, we are also very much jumping into the action above water. Wakanda is going to be forced to bust out the Wakandan Navy, which we'll be seeing for the first time. The Royal Sea Leopard is a giant Helicarrier-style ship that will allow the Wakandans to bring some of their technology under the depths to fight these new foes. There's a breadth of new vehicles in Wakanda that we'll get to see in action, much like the Royal Talon Fighters and the Dragon Fliers from the first film. We are figuring out the visual effects that will help breathe life into the Wakanda Navy, in particular the new Sunbird, which is a cool air vehicle that plays very much in the film.

Ruth Carter (Costume Designer):

For the Wakandan Navy, we used a palette of green, since the River Tribe uses green, and Egyptian line work for the armor. We also wanted to show ranking in a different way, so we did a septum ring as representing a certain rank. We did a septum to the ear chain as another rank. It's something that you don't normally see. We really wanted to give them a sense of Wakandan royalty as well, so we brought in gold and silver as an accent color.

Ruth Carter has designed costumes for more than 40 movies in her career. In 2019, she won the Academy Award for Achievement in Costume Design for *Marvel Studios' Black Panther*, making history as the first African American to win in the category. She talks to us now.

RUTH CARTER
(COSTUME DESIGNER)

"All of the costumes have a color story, so each has their own power. Of course, Angela Bassett could wear a ten-gallon hat and still make it work!"

Did you discuss the influences from Mayan culture?

We had lots of meetings in preparation—three times a week, everybody together, guided by our historians. We wanted to make this as accurate as possible, with intriguing details that we wouldn't think of without help from the historians. For instance, the snake image is very important to the Mayan culture. But we were also creating a new world, a subculture that has lived underwater for thousands of years, which gave us more latitude. We also met with marine experts to talk about what could be found at that depth, 1,500 feet below sea level. We were given a whole list of things that we could use to create costumes and elements for the Talokanil.

Our instinct was to use feathers, since they are associated with the Maya, but our little community of Mayans don't have a lot of feathers. We used shells more than feathers. There is some feather work underwater because a lot of fish fins do look feathery and colorful. But there's a defining point where you don't want it to start looking too Aztec. The Aztec civilization was much bigger, much more elaborate. And as soon as you start using feathers in your headdresses then you start breaching that line. We were connected all the time with the historians. I'd send them pictures and ask questions: Is this a good direction or not?

What is your process for creating costumes?

We use 3-D printing, so we have to do a lot of careful measurements. We don't use anything that's bought at a store. So our measurements are super important. We make prototypes to understand how big or how small we want things. For Ramonda, for example, we would use the earlier crowns [to gauge scale]. Wig work will also change measurements. All of this is discussed and put into play before we create the final version. Then we do several fittings, working with cutters who make her outfits. I do a lot of illustrations and we all talk about what can be shown in which setting. We have a color story going, even for the white that Ramonda wears.

RUTH CARTER'S COSTUMES RANGED FROM PRACTICAL OUTFITS (*ABOVE TOP*) TO REGAL DRESS AND MILITARY UNIFORMS (*ABOVE*).

All of the costumes have a color story, so each has their own power. Of course, Angela Bassett could wear a ten-gallon hat and still make it work!

Talk us through Namor's overall design.
He's King Namor, so his costume reflect that regal aspect, and the culture he comes from. Also, it reflects the look of the character from the comics. His shoulder mantle was curated from post-Yucatec Mayan cultures, using snake symbols. We also incorporated the look of kelp in the headdress. His cape was hand woven and we added shells and beads to it. His looks give you a sense that he has traveled through time. He has one drape that he wears underneath his arm and over his shoulder, which feels very Roman or Grecian. He's able to get away with it because he has lived through the ages. We're showing that he has a story to tell—the story of his life and the growth of this world.

How did you costume the Wakandans for water?
Well, the Dora Milaje costume in the first film, for

ABOVE: COSTUMES FOR NAMORA AND SHURI'S BLACK PANTHER.

M'BAKU'S COSTUME UTILIZES AN ARMORED BREASTPLATE AND SPIKED FOREARM GUARDS.

example, was made of leather, and leather and water are not friends. So we took the original costume and made a mold of it. Then it was painted to look like leather so that it could get wet—all the neck rings and arm rings, and the beaded aspects, were re-created so they could stand getting wet: They weren't made of metal, beads, wood or leather. That way we wouldn't end up ruining the costumes from the first movie, which we wanted to keep for historic and archival purposes.

Do you ever have a chance to see your costumes on the monitor?

I get a chance to stop and look at things on the monitor for ten minutes. After the first shot, I can generally kind of feel good that it's there, it's landed. Then I have to rush off to work on things that are coming up. This is a big film with a lot of layers, and a lot of things that we had to accomplish. We were coming from all different points. Namor's big headdress was built in New Zealand. We had things that were made in India. Queen Ramonda's pieces were beaded outside of the country.

How do you keep timing together with all the disparate elements?

The schedule makes everybody crazy because it can change on a dime based on an actor's availability, or on the timing for a set depending on how things have to be built. We're constantly talking about scheduling, and things do dramatically change that creates a rush in our department—but we never can't do it. We always figure out how we can get it to camera in time. Sometimes, the energy of coming up with something at the last minute is exhilarating.

What has this franchise meant to you?

It's definitely a career highlight. Presenting African culture in a futuristic way without the impact of colonization is a high concept. It's a joy to see what it's meant for people who want to dress like Okoye, or a Dora, at Halloween, or to be the Black Panther. It was a joy to see children embodying something that was so positive and that would bring them a sense of pride, self-assurance, and confidence.

CARTER BASED QUEEN RAMONDA'S CROWNS ON TRADITIONAL ZULU HEADDRESSES.

MARVEL STUDIOS LIBRARY

MOVIE SPECIALS
- MARVEL STUDIOS' *SPIDER-MAN FAR FROM HOME*
- MARVEL STUDIOS' *ANT-MAN AND THE WASP*
- MARVEL STUDIOS' *AVENGERS: ENDGAME*
- MARVEL STUDIOS' *AVENGERS: INFINITY WAR*
- MARVEL STUDIOS' *BLACK PANTHER* (COMPANION)
- MARVEL STUDIOS' *BLACK WIDOW*
- MARVEL STUDIOS' *CAPTAIN MARVEL*
- MARVEL STUDIOS: THE FIRST TEN YEARS
- MARVEL STUDIOS' *THOR: RAGNAROK*
- MARVEL STUDIOS' *AVENGERS: AN INSIDER'S GUIDE TO THE AVENGERS' FILMS*
- MARVEL STUDIOS' *WANDAVISION*
- MARVEL STUDIOS' *THE FALCON AND THE WINTER SOLDIER*

MARVEL STUDIOS' LOKI: THE OFFICIAL MARVEL STUDIOS COLLECTOR SPECIAL

MARVEL STUDIOS' ETERNALS THE OFFICIAL MARVEL STUDIOS MOVIE SPECIAL

MARVEL STUDIOS' SPIDER-MAN: NO WAY HOME THE OFFICIAL MOVIE SPECIAL

MARVEL STUDIOS' DOCTOR STRANGE IN THE MULTIVERSE OF MADNESS THE OFFICIAL MOVIE SPECIAL

MARVEL STUDIOS' HAWKEYE: THE OFFICIAL MARVEL STUDIOS COLLECTOR SPECIAL

MARVEL LEGACY LIBRARY

MARVEL'S AVENGERS BLACK PANTHER: WAR FOR WAKANDA: THE ART OF THE EXPANSION

MARVEL'S CAPTAIN AMERICA: THE FIRST 80 YEARS

MARVEL: THE FIRST 80 YEARS

MARVEL'S DEADPOOL: THE FIRST 60 YEARS

MARVEL'S FANTASTIC FOUR: THE FIRST 60 YEARS

MARVEL'S SPIDER-MAN: THE FIRST 60 YEARS

MARVEL CLASSIC NOVELS
- WOLVERINE WEAPON X OMNIBUS
- SPIDER-MAN THE DARKEST HOURS OMNIBUS
- SPIDER-MAN THE VENOM FACTOR OMNIBUS
- X-MEN AND THE AVENGERS GAMMA QUEST OMNIBUS
- X-MEN MUTANT EMPIRE OMNIBUS

NOVELS
- MARVEL'S GUARDIANS OF THE GALAXY NO GUTS, NO GLORY
- SPIDER-MAN MILES MORALES WINGS OF FURY
- MORBIUS THE LIVING VAMPIRE: BLOOD TIES
- ANT-MAN NATURAL ENEMY
- AVENGERS EVERYBODY WANTS TO RULE THE WORLD

- AVENGERS INFINITY
- BLACK PANTHER WHO IS THE BLACK PANTHER?
- CAPTAIN AMERICA DARK DESIGNS
- CAPTAIN MARVEL LIBERATION RUN
- CIVIL WAR
- DEADPOOL PAWS
- SPIDER-MAN FOREVER YOUNG
- SPIDER-MAN KRAVEN'S LAST HUNT
- THANOS DEATH SENTENCE
- VENOM LETHAL PROTECTOR
- X-MEN DAYS OF FUTURE PAST
- X-MEN THE DARK PHOENIX SAGA
- SPIDER-MAN HOSTILE TAKEOVER

ART BOOKS
- *THE GUARDIANS OF THE GALAXY* THE ART OF THE GAME
- MARVEL'S AVENGERS: *BLACK PANTHER: WAR FOR WAKANDA* THE ART OF THE EXPANSION
- MARVEL'S *SPIDER-MAN MILES MORALES* THE ART OF THE GAME
- MARVEL'S *AVENGERS* THE ART OF THE GAME
- MARVEL'S *SPIDER-MAN* THE ART OF THE GAME
- MARVEL *CONTEST OF CHAMPIONS* THE ART OF THE BATTLEREALM
- *SPIDER-MAN: INTO THE SPIDER-VERSE* THE ART OF THE MOVIE
- *THE ART OF IRON MAN* THE ART OF THE MOVIE

STAR WARS LIBRARY

STAR WARS: THE MANDALORIAN GUIDE TO SEASON ONE

STAR WARS: THE MANDALORIAN GUIDE TO SEASON TWO

STAR WARS: THE EMPIRE STRIKES BACK: THE 40TH ANNIVERSARY SPECIAL EDITION

STAR WARS INSIDER: THE FICTION COLLECTION VOLUME 2

STAR WARS: THE SKYWALKER SAGA THE OFFICIAL COLLECTOR'S EDITION

STAR WARS THE HIGH REPUBLIC STARLIGHT STORIES

- *ROGUE ONE: A STAR WARS STORY* THE OFFICIAL COLLECTOR'S EDITION
- *ROGUE ONE: A STAR WARS STORY* THE OFFICIAL MISSION DEBRIEF
- *STAR WARS: THE LAST JEDI* THE OFFICIAL COLLECTOR'S EDITION
- *STAR WARS: THE LAST JEDI* THE OFFICIAL MOVIE COMPANION
- *STAR WARS: THE LAST JEDI* THE ULTIMATE GUIDE
- *SOLO: A STAR WARS STORY* THE OFFICIAL COLLECTOR'S EDITION
- *SOLO: A STAR WARS STORY* THE ULTIMATE GUIDE
- THE BEST OF *STAR WARS INSIDER* VOLUME 1

- THE BEST OF *STAR WARS INSIDER* VOLUME 2
- THE BEST OF *STAR WARS INSIDER* VOLUME 3
- THE BEST OF *STAR WARS INSIDER* VOLUME 4
- *STAR WARS:* LORDS OF THE SITH
- *STAR WARS:* HEROES OF THE FORCE
- *STAR WARS:* ICONS OF THE GALAXY
- *STAR WARS:* THE SAGA BEGINS
- *STAR WARS* THE ORIGINAL TRILOGY
- *STAR WARS:* ROGUES, SCOUNDRELS AND BOUNTY HUNTERS
- *STAR WARS:* CREATURES, ALIENS, AND DROIDS
- *STAR WARS: THE RISE OF SKYWALKER* THE OFFICIAL COLLECTOR'S EDITION

- *STAR WARS: THE MANDALORIAN:* GUIDE TO SEASON ONE
- *STAR WARS: THE MANDALORIAN:* GUIDE TO SEASON TWO
- *STAR WARS: THE EMPIRE STRIKES BACK* THE 40TH ANNIVERSARY SPECIAL EDITION
- *STAR WARS: AGE OF RESISTANCE* THE OFFICIAL COLLECTORS' EDITION
- *STAR WARS: THE SKYWALKER SAGA* THE OFFICIAL COLLECTOR'S EDITION
- *STAR WARS INSIDER: FICTION COLLECTION* VOLUME 1
- *STAR WARS INSIDER PRESENTS: MANDALORIAN SEASON 2* VOLUME 1
- *STAR WARS INSIDER PRESENTS: MANDALORIAN SEASON 2* VOLUME 2

AVAILABLE AT ALL GOOD BOOKSTORES AND ONLINE

TITAN-COMICS.COM | TITANBOOKS.COM